Story, Ritual, Prophecy, Wisdom

STORY
RITUAL
PROPHECY
WISDOM

Reading and Teaching the Bible Today

Mark W. Hamilton and Samjung Kang-Hamilton

WILLIAM B. EERDMANS PUBLISHING COMPANY

Grand Rapids, Michigan

Wm. B. Eerdmans Publishing Co.
4035 Park East Court SE, Grand Rapids, Michigan 49546
www.eerdmans.com

Book design by Jamie McKee

Printed in the United States of America

30 29 28 27 26 25 24   1 2 3 4 5 6 7

ISBN 978-0-8028-8318-6

Library of Congress Cataloging-in-Publication Data

A catalog record for this book is available from the Library of Congress.

For Bob and in memory of Jan

Contents

Preface

This book began its life almost by accident about twenty years ago around our kitchen table with our then young children running around as children do. We planned to teach a class bringing together our respective disciplines, Hebrew Bible/Old Testament and Christian religious education/formation. The slashes are significant. Each of us inhabits an academic discipline that values contact with many others and seeks to serve the larger community. Now we were trying to fashion yet another interdisciplinary dialogue at least among ourselves and prospective students.

As the years have passed, we have taught that course over and over. The students have changed. Fewer of them today see their future careers marked out for them by established congregations. Few wear denominational loyalty on their sleeves, though anxiety-ridden relationships with their heritages have also diminished. More women are coming to the fore, and the boundaries between predominantly White and predominantly minoritized congregations have come to seem less acceptable, less "natural." The hesitant and searching attitude evident in our classroom has presaged a period of creativity and the first signs of renewal.

In part, this book comes out of our classroom experiences. It also reflects a longer life of engagement with churches in places where we served together in ministry in several forms (preaching, pastoring, chairing congregational education committees, writing church curricula, teaching Sunday school for children and adults, participating in small groups and in campus ministry). We have lived in South Korea, Texas, Arkansas, Connecticut, and Massachusetts, and have found friends in ministry in Singapore, Croatia, and across the United States. We have spoken in congregations and gatherings of church leaders many times over the past few decades. So we speak as insiders, albeit insiders uncomfortable with the status quo and looking for something more hopeful and life-giving.

The thousands of thoughtful questions from those we have met have sharpened our thinking. A book can never replicate a seminary course, a sermon, or a church workshop, and should not attempt to. Yet it can always draw together experiences and ideas contributing to an argument. That is the case here.

In writing this work, we have accumulated many debts, first of all to each other, and then to friends. We thank the churches in which we have worked in ministry, especially the New Milford (Connecticut) Church of Christ, who welcomed us as newlyweds in our first ministry appointment over thirty years ago, and the Brookline (Massachusetts) Church of Christ, who helped us find an adult faith in trying times. We also thank the many congregations in which we have taught over the past several decades, especially the University Church of Christ in Abilene, Texas. The hospitality of many individuals and congregations continues to remind us of the greater hospitality of the Lord they serve.

In our life together, a few persons have stood out for their friendship and their example. Chief among them are our friends Bob and Jan Randolph. Bob has ministered for decades with the Brookline Church of Christ, where he has mentored scores of young women and men who serve the church and the world with distinction. He was the first chaplain to the Institute at the Massachusetts Institute of Technology. He models for us and countless others around the world what it means to be a model of peace and justice, in short, a Christian, in a diverse environment that welcomed open dialogue and encouraged serious theological questions. His life partner Jan, whose untimely death we mourn, was a mainstay at Brookline and at Harvard's Memorial Church, where she worked as executive assistant to the pastor and Plummer Professor of Christian Morals, Peter Gomes. Her contributions go far deeper than the job title would imply.

Bob and Jan showed us what a Christian married couple could look like. This was never clearer than during Jan's last months, as Bob cared for her with the tenderness and dedication that models for us what the Hebrew Bible calls *hesed*, steadfast love. We dedicate this book to them with the deepest gratitude and affection.

CHAPTER 1

The Bible and Christian Formation
in Contemporary Contexts

In his extraordinary book about Gentiles who rescued Jews during the
Holocaust, Sir Martin Gilbert recounts the story of David Prital, who
found refuge among a small Ukrainian Baptist sect. He had sought them
out on advice from a friendly German coachman. On meeting the poor
Baptist farmer in his field, Prital entered his modest home, each man
knowing who the other was. Prital remembers:

> "God brought an important guest to our house," he said to his wife.
> "We should thank God for this blessing." They knelt down and I
> heard a wonderful prayer coming out of their pure and simple hearts,
> not written in a single prayer book. I heard a song addressed to God,
> thanking God for the opportunity to meet a son of Israel in these crazy
> days. . . . They stopped praying and we sat down at the table for a meal,
> which was enjoyable. The peasant's wife gave us milk and potatoes.
> Before the meal, the master of the house read a chapter from the Bible.
> Here it is, I thought, this is the big secret. It is this eternal book that
> raised their morality to such unbelievable heights. It is this very book
> that filled their hearts with love for the Jews.[1]

A modest meal. A heartfelt prayer. Courage and honor. It's an edifying
story. Under extreme duress, at the risk of their lives, two people take
to heart the message of Scripture and act on it.

Yet almost immediately doubts arise. What about those who read
the Bible and did nothing, or worse, joined the killers? What about

---

1. Martin Gilbert, *The Righteous: The Unsung Heroes of the Holocaust* (New York:
Holt, 2003), 13.

those like an Oskar Schindler, who could not be accused of excessive piety, but rescued hundreds of lives? Does the "big secret" really lurk in the best-selling book of all time? Or is something beyond the mere act of exposure needed? While the Bible can inspire spiritual courage, generosity, and love for enemies and strangers, it does not always do so. How do we make sense of the difference?

We are writing our own book at a time when serious questions have arisen about the place of the Bible in the contemporary world and even in the church. Pastors and professors lament biblical illiteracy,[2] though for different reasons. For some, the problem arises when ignorance of the Good Book robs us of an understanding of Western art, music, literature, and the world of ideas precisely when all that seems most vulnerable to the manipulations of Big Tech and Wall Street. Something called Christian culture, which does not require faith in God, is at risk. For others, the problem goes deeper. Ignorance of the Bible robs us of God and morality and eventually humanity itself. The end of religious practice would mean, not the beginning of utopia, but the end of the pursuit of justice. In a world without religious texts, there will be *Mein Kampf*s ready to fill the void.

At the same time, many people wonder if the Bible is not itself a less turgid and more artful, but for all that even more dangerous, ancestor of Hitler's ravings. Does it really foster a life of goodness and mercy, or does it provide a warrant for some of the most heinous human behaviors, from the Crusades to the persecution of ethnic or sexual minorities? Can the church be a community of virtue if it continues its intense engagement with this book? Is Holy Writ really holy? A world where all sorts of ideas clash in the public arena challenges anyone writing about the Bible to face the book and its readers with eyes open.

As teachers of the Hebrew Bible or Old Testament (Mark) and Christian religious education (Samjung), we wish to engage these questions. Virtually every year over the past two decades, we have conducted a course together helping pastoral leaders teach Scripture in contemporary contexts. That course draws on our separate research agendas plus

---

2. Two excellent examples are Brent A. Strawn, *The Old Testament Is Dying: A Diagnosis and Recommended Treatment* (Grand Rapids: Baker Academic, 2017); and John Goldingay, *Reading Jesus's Bible: How the New Testament Helps Us Understand the Old Testament* (Grand Rapids: Eerdmans, 2017).

now three decades of ministry in several forms, for Samjung first as a missions researcher and Christian educator in her native South Korea, and then for both Mark and Samjung in various parts of the United States. Our joint effort tries to connect biblical studies and Christian religious education.

We have no interest in writing a jeremiad longing for a lost time that never was. Nor do we want to live as Pollyannas bubbling good cheer. Biblical illiteracy has always challenged the church and the culture beyond it. As we have seen in our travels, church leaders face this problem all over the Christian world, whether the health and wealth gospel in the Global South or the semisecularism of the church in the Global North. Worse, some forms of knowing Scripture have often allowed its domestication, so that even the rawest, most challenging words come to bolster an unjust system. Leaders can simultaneously announce the imminent end of the world and ask for money to pay for that announcement.

In short, neither praising an ideal past nor groaning over a fallen present or threatening future will help us. Conversely, times of challenge often awaken creativity. Now is the time to reflect on the state of teaching and learning in the church, particularly with respect to the Bible. Now is the time to learn and unlearn.

In this book, then, we argue that the Bible's diversity and interconnectedness offer a model for the church's encounter with it. A gift from past generations of Israelite prophets, Jewish sages, and Jesus-following apostles, this text comes to us requiring interpretation. Meaning-making requires not just the text but also the reader, and the complex encounter of the two requires our imagination and self-examination. It also requires a ritualized life, the practice of worship that draws on the biblical texts as resources, and that life, in turn, requires a community. Biblical interpretation always occurs in a community cultivating wisdom and pursuing justice and peace. Otherwise, it goes badly awry. Mark's work has concentrated on the biblical text and its afterlife in faith communities. Samjung's research has explored the dynamics of Christian formation in churches across cultures and in multicultural settings, as well as the art of teaching for transformation.

Together, we remain convinced that the stories, prophecies, poems, and laws of ancient Israel and the early church deserve the most intense and creative engagement precisely because that engagement promotes

human well-being. That engagement does not require passive acceptance of every conviction an ancient text might have, but it does require
of us something more than the hermeneutics of suspicion. For example,
in recognizing that the Bible does not always overcome the patriarchal
views of antiquity we ought not simply hand the texts over to those
who value them precisely because they seek to preserve patriarchy.
Since patriarchy is an unstable set of practices, beliefs, and values, all of
which are contestable both in biblical times and later, we ought to find
the ways in which these texts question and probe the limits of social
structures. When we do, we find much value. The same goes for other
sets of -isms we might identify. We call upon the church to try to bring
adults, teenagers, and children into the world the Bible imagines, while
understanding the one it describes.

The Bible was not created to validate human structures, ancient or
modern. No true prophet ever celebrated what already existed. Quite the
opposite. The Bible consistently disrupts easy confidence in all human
structures, calling readers to imagine alternatives. In this world that
the Bible evokes, all things human are provisional and contingent upon
God's mercy.

We realize that our questioning of limitless questioning will encourage some readers to doubt our commitment to justice-oriented readings
of the Bible. Since all readings are contestable, plausibly or implausibly,
it is probably impossible to prevent such a stance toward our work. Yet
we take heart from a brilliant essay by the Queer theorist Eve Kosofsky Sedgwick, beautifully entitled "Paranoid Reading and Reparative
Reading, or, You're So Paranoid, You Probably Think This Essay Is about
You."[3] She notes that in many forms of literary criticism—and certainly
this is true of some parts of biblical studies—"paranoia has by now
candidly become less a diagnosis than a prescription."[4] The question is
not whether we recognize systemic oppression here and there, since
no thinking person can fail to see that, but how we respond to it. The
paranoid reading style anticipates problems, protecting the reader
from the text by assuming that its negative dimensions not just exist
but can overpower and harm. And, she continues, paranoia "places its

---

3. Eve Kosofsky Sedgwick, *Touching Feeling: Affect, Pedagogy, Performativity*
(Durham, NC: Duke University Press, 2003), 123–51.
4. Kosofsky Sedgwick, *Touching Feeling*, 125.

faith in exposure."[5] Yet exposure alone does not help us move beyond a defensive stance.

The paranoid style of reading flourishes in some corners of biblical studies and practical theology. All of us reading the Bible face choices made by prior readers (or community of readers). Suspicion may protect the reader from textual violence, but it may also protect us from surprise, wonder, and true learning. We may end up confusing the oppressed with the oppressor, the questioner with the proclaimer, and the outsider with the powerful insider. Suspicion sees the text as an enemy, at least potentially.

The detour taken just now will stymie some readers who have encountered biblical studies in some of its more conservative forms. We take their need for a liberative reading of Scripture seriously. We do not seek to import a conservative approach to the Bible by the back door because the Bible is often a radical book, a disruptive and life-seeking book.

So, we are willing to risk misunderstanding from several directions, in part because today all serious biblical scholars, Christian religious educators, theologians, and pastors struggle to find language to talk about the Bible, or indeed theology more generally. Even the most self-effacing and harmless words have been weaponized by this group or that, put to work building ramparts and digging ditches so that our camp may defend itself from yours. The near obsession with words in all wings of the theological academy, left and right, has led us to a point where, paradoxically, we can barely communicate with each other without providing a list of "approved" definitions of terms, and even more challengingly, the proper combination of them. Many of us, regardless of our theological family, find ourselves locked in intramural theological conversations that seem more about building group solidarity than about discovering new insights or building new relationships. Still, we must take our chances and hope that at least some readers will make allowances for the brokenness of our language. We will struggle to find the right words, and if that struggle stimulates disputation, then all the better. Out of the clash of ideas, new understandings will arise.

In writing this work, then, we acknowledge our own situatedness in a particular corner of North America, of the church, and of social

---

5. Kosofsky Sedgwick, *Touching Feeling*, 138–39.

settings more generally. We can only speak about what we know, and invite others to join the conversation. We are of different sexes, cultures of origin, and first languages. We were trained in different disciplines. Yet we have lived together as a married couple with two children (now adults) for more than three decades in several parts of the United States with certain friends, enjoying some things and not others, believing some things and not others. We have learned to challenge each other to find deeper levels of truth, while respecting each other's right to think differently. We have learned to communicate with each other because we have worked at it.

Our situatedness is real, and it shapes how we think, undoubtedly in both negative and positive ways. We share the reality of our particularity with others in their particularity. The one thing we human beings have in common is the fact that our commonality always coexists with our differences. The paradox makes us human. We do not agree either that our particularity is so decisive that it cannot be understood or questioned by others, or conversely, that our similarities should put our distinctions into the shade. Communication must always cross boundaries, and we must respect both the boundaries and the act of crossing them.

If we acknowledge that paradox, then we must leave open the possibility that Prital's story of devout rescuers can be more than a pretty tale of highly exceptional people. While we hope never to need the sort of courage the Ukrainian Baptists exhibited (since we hope never to replicate the events that required it), we should ask how to imitate their ethical clarity and will to help. And to our specific point, is there anything about the Bible that would foster the sort of moral courage, and even joy, that appears in this story?

In this book, we try to make a simple, yet challenging case. At the moment, many of our churches, regardless of denomination or theological stance, experience a growing distance from their own texts and traditions. At the same time, the church seems increasingly irrelevant to more and more people. These two facts are related because the church has little to offer beyond its vision of God, humanity, and the created world articulated in the Bible and in the definitive creeds and traditions that derive from it.

The church's growing irrelevance does not come from its lag behind the latest moves of the dominant media culture. It comes from our ignorance of our own heritage and identity. With rare exceptions, we have not sufficiently attended to the relationship between the life of faith and the contemporary contexts in which individuals and religious communities exist. Yes, today's many kinds of pluralisms and anti-pluralisms, the omnipresence of the market economy, the reconfiguration of family and community in the West, and the decay of traditional denominational loyalties, all make it necessary for us to rethink how and why we teach Scripture. Yet the answer does not come from going with the flow and uncritically embracing every cultural development. We need to relearn how Scripture can be an interpretive tool by which we make sense of our lives, as well as a norming text (canon) by which we judge our own behaviors and commitments as Christians.

The internal challenges facing churches in the United States stem from the surrounding context, in which massive cultural shifts have impacted many younger people and led many older people to a stance of extreme reaction. Our news feeds populate with pictures of white-haired congregants voting themselves out of denominations as a way of fighting the culture wars. At the same time, we see the widespread disinterest of young adults in the church's adult educational programs, as many of our practices of youth ministry have orphaned successive generations.

Likewise, the facile identification of Christianity with nationalism has infected conservative churches especially, but the resulting moral embarrassment has tarred most Christians with the same brush. As a friend told us recently, when others ask her whether she is a Christian she always replies with, "You tell me what you mean by 'Christian,' and I'll tell you if I am one." There is a widespread sense, especially among young adults, even those whose parents and grandparents practiced Christian faith in depth, that an unbridgeable chasm stretches between the life and teachings of Jesus and the practices of the church. So there is deep unrest, even among those who answer the pollster's question, "what religion are you?," with the label "Christian." We find ourselves in the eye of the perfect storm.

From Problem to Solution

The good news is that many thinkers across the Christian theological spectrum (as well as others) are writing to address the same problems, and we owe many of them a great debt. Proposals for the church's renewal come from many directions, bearing such labels as the emerging church, new monasticism, simple church, hybrid church, online or digital church, Brown church, organic church, missional church, and on and on. Despite these differences, all these movements share in common a sense that a post-Christian age has emerged in the Global North, the historic home of Christianity.

They also all refuse to follow the path of cultural accommodation pursued by both some liberal Protestants in the 1960s (as exemplified in such bestsellers as the *Secular City* and *Honest to God*[6]) and many fundamentalist Protestants in the 1980s (as in Focus on the Family and the Moral Majority, which despite their anticultural rhetoric usually embraced right-wing economics and politics). In other words, the church's failure to discern its own position in the broader cultural landscape cuts across tribes.

The new voices of renewal often reclaim some part of the premodern Christian tradition, either in theology or spiritual practices or both. And for most of them, the old denominational fissures that emerged in North America in the absence of state churches or in Europe with them, no longer hold sway. A deep-seated ecumenism is taking hold, even as the old structures (especially in Protestantism) disintegrate.

It is difficult to know how much the renewal work of contemporary theologians has trickled down to the life of congregations and their members. At its best, that work creatively fashions out of old texts and practices new and vibrant ways of being Christian today. Whether the best theology, or even good-enough theology, gets a hearing will depend on local pastors and teachers. Theirs is the voice we are trying to tune.

We want to espouse a generous solution to the problem of the church's distance from its own texts in order to reflect the generosity of God. Such a stance lies at the heart of all proper Christian theology. We believe that truly ecumenical theological work requires both a firm commitment to a set of identifiable ideas and a willingness to listen carefully and appreciatively to those whose views differ. In the twin acts of listening and speaking, we can together grow in our understanding. We will also value each other more.

---

6. Harvey Cox, *The Secular City* (Princeton: Princeton University Press, 2013); John Robinson, *Honest to God*, 50th anniversary ed. (London: SCM, 2013).

Every year, the American Bible Society publishes its *State of the Bible* report. It documents a downward trend in readership, even though the Bible remains by far the most widely read single book in North America. The most recent data seems to show, as the researchers put it, "that many Americans are struggling to connect the teaching of the Bible to the ways they live out their faith in community."[7] The most puzzling part of that longitudinal study may be the high percentage of people who own a Bible, value it as divine revelation in some way, but read it only occasionally, perhaps in a time of crisis. It is easy to explain why a person who fervently believes that the Bible, however interpreted, speaks for God also believes that it therefore demands constant study. It is also easy to understand someone who regards the Bible as boring and therefore never touches it, or as dangerous, and therefore reads it with the intent of exposing its evils. It is not easy to understand why someone believes the book to be divine in origin but never feels compelled to read it. That cognitive gap must come from somewhere. We could lament, as the American Bible Society researchers do, the loss of a "biblical worldview," or put in a more sophisticated way, a theologically informed Christian stance toward the world. But such a lament may well miss the point. In our view, the current widespread cognitive dissonance derives from the way churches teach the Bible, either as a book of rules or as a grab bag of vaguely heart-warming memes. No sensible person would work up the emotional commitment needed for serious engagement with such a text.

Perhaps, then, we need to come at the solution from some basic theological commitments. For Christians, the starting point must be the nature of God as a merciful creator and sustainer of the universe, including human beings. Christians should trust the ongoing creative work of God in healing and reconciling all things so that they retain their created status as distinct yet interconnected beings. Christians believe that God is manifested in the life and work of Jesus Christ, the God-man who revealed to us both God's nature and our own. All our reading of Scripture keeps in mind that underlying preunderstanding of our existence. All our teaching must reflect God's mercy as well.

7. Jeffery Fulks, Randy Petersen, and John Farquhar Plake, eds., *State of the Bible USA 2022: Research from American Bible Society* (Philadelphia: American Bible Society, 2022), xvii.

Proceeding Forward

Still, preunderstandings or underlying assumptions cannot provide an adequate approach to reading the Bible for its life-giving potential. We need more. In this volume, we will lay out our argument in several steps. Chapters 2–6 will explore the nature of the Bible, as a taught book (chapter 2). We will then explore what we call the modes of Scripture, or its primary uses in the church's life of teaching and learning (chapters 3–6). These modes are narrative, ritual, prophecy, and wisdom (including law). Those labels both describe the literary genres involved and the needs that the church has as a community that lives out a narrative, celebrates and mourns, critically examines itself and the world, and fosters patterns of life that cohere and invigorate.

We then move toward an understanding of our context and a reimagining of teaching in it (chapter 7). Culture is not a static entity that one either accepts or rejects. Nor, conversely, is it simply a grab bag of options from which sovereign individuals choose preferred behaviors without reference to anyone else. Rather, culture is a dynamic cluster of practices, values, beliefs, and feelings that individuals and groups engage with varying degrees of intentionality, self-awareness, and empathy. The reimagining of the church's place in the landscape of North America will undoubtedly require more skill than we have, but we hope to find at least the first traces of a path forward.

This final move also involves models for transformational teaching and learning and a rethinking of the role of the teacher. Art implies more than technique, however sophisticated. If teaching is an art, what is the artifact created? Surely, it is the student's life. The teacher's tools may include lecture and discussion, of course, but it may also include the arts (music, painting, sculpture, film, digital media), case teaching, storytelling, *lectio divina*, and so on. The teaching of Scripture demands that we leave behind the Sunday school and embrace a much wider set of experiences.

In our journey through our parts of the worldwide church, we have shared life with a great host of honest seekers who all wish their religious traditions, including the Christian church, to be harbingers of hope, mercy, grace, and peace. Those are not mere clichés. They are commitments. We hope that this book will provide those fellow travelers with, if not a guide to the path ahead, at least the voice of a companion on the road.

CHAPTER 2

The Bible as a Taught Text

In this volume, we explore four modalities of Scripture: narrative, ritual, prophecy, and wisdom. These categories are broad literary ones, covering a range of genres and subgenres. More crucially, they also denote the work these texts do in faith communities. We will claim that the diversity of the Christian or Jewish canons reflects the need of those communities to make sense of their life before God. In other words, literature serves purposes, and genres live in their performance. This multilayered understanding of the biblical text and its life in communities, families, and individuals pursuing Christian faith will drive our discussion.

Yet a prior issue also needs addressing. What is the Bible and what is it for? For some people, this question will seem odd: the Bible is an ancient book sold in every bookstore, nicely printed and bound together. It has its own ISBN, and there are thousands of books about it. The academic game of identifying something already well known seems just that, a game.

However, different communities who read the Bible in worship every week disagree about which books go in it. Though agreeing on most topics, they disagree about what sort of authority it has and over which areas of life.

In this chapter, then, we will stake out a location in the landscape of theological reflections on the nature and use of the Bible. We will take bearings in two dimensions, the theological meanings of Scripture (its authority and generativity) and its uses in the formational practices of the church. Our discussion is inevitably brief and sketchy, open to further conversation in many directions. Such a reconnoiter cannot equate to occupation of the full territory. We invite further reflection from all sides.

God's Book?

The consensus of the church over centuries has been that the Bible comes somehow from God as a gift. In this view, the words of the text have efficacy in the lives of a religious community and individuals. These assumptions go back to the very beginning of the Christian tradition and indeed into Second Temple Judaism (the period 539 BCE–70 CE). Debates about what given texts mean or even which texts count as Scripture have existed throughout the past two thousand years or so, but those debates concerned the practical implications of texts whose importance was beyond question.

The relevant texts in the New Testament accept (bolster, even create) that consensus by rooting notions of the relevance and efficacy of the church's scriptures in its most salient theological ideas and religious experiences. As the first epistle of Peter put it, probably near the end of the first century CE:

> About this salvation the prophets, prophesying about the grace extended to you, explored and investigated the matter, searching at what sort of time Christ's spirit would reveal the thing witnessed in advance, the sufferings related to Christ and the accompanying glorious things. To them, it was revealed that it was not for themselves but for you that they were serving, through those things now proclaimed to you, which were brought you by those announcing to you what they were told by the Holy Spirit sent from heaven (which angels hankered to look at). (1 Pet 1:10–12)[1]

This complex text positions its readers as recipients of ancient, holy promises whose fulfillment was guaranteed by God, announced by both ancient prophets and more recent missionaries. It also understands the prophets (which would include not just Isaiah and Amos, but David and Moses, as commonly thought in ancient Judaism), to be proclaimers of ultimate hope for human beings, not only as social critics. For 1 Peter, the implied audience of the letter equaled the implied audience of the prophets, the "you" who sought redemption from Israel's God. These older figures do not appear simply as imaginative geniuses but as

---

1. All translations are the authors' own.

conduits of the divine imagination. The already old Scriptures become, for the author of this epistle, windows into ultimate meaning.

A more formulaic but no less instructive text appears in the (probably later) epistle 2 Timothy, in which the writer addresses the recipient this way:

> You, remain with the things you have learned and understood, knowing about the things you've learned. From childhood, you have known the holy writings, the powerful things you have become wise about for salvation through the faith that is in Christ Jesus. Every Scripture is God-breathed and profitable for teaching, for reproof, for correction, for formation for justice, so that the person belonging to God might be fully qualified, skilled at every good work. (2 Tim 3:14–17)

The character "Timothy," the implied first reader of the text, should recall the whole set of life experiences that led him to his life as a Christ-follower. At the center of those experiences lay the Scriptures of Israel, which provided language for "salvation," the robust idea of God's unexpected, uncontrolled, unearned acts of mercy that reclaim and renew broken or aimless human lives. The work the scriptural texts do includes a moral reformation ("reproof, correction") in order to direct a life toward justice, an imitation of the activities of God.

Fundamentalist Christians often start their reflections on the nature and authority of the Bible with this text to anchor their theology in a very high (as they see it) notion of divine inspiration. Yet 2 Timothy does not explain what it means by "God-breathed" (*theopneustos*) except to say that the origin of the Scriptures and the orientation of its readers both have everything to do with God. Scripture is part of the created order, and therefore an expression of divine grace. How it is so does not concern this text except with regard to the consequences in the lives of the maturing believers and church community as a whole.

These texts and others think of the church's Bible, which was still growing as the ink was drying on 2 Timothy and 1 Peter, as a coherent collection whose full meaning can only become clear in view of God's commitment to bring wholeness to humanity, or in other words, God's grace. The entire Christian Bible, Old and New Testaments, is suffused with a sense of the divine presence everywhere in the cosmos. For the New Testament authors, the ultimate revelation of that presence is the person of Jesus Christ. Those who embrace that understanding of reality, mediated to them also by the prophetic words, begin to live just and verdant lives. (And the absence of justice would, conversely, be a sign of misunderstanding or rebellion in those claiming to be Christian.)

This broad consensus, already emerging in the New Testament, grew over time as Christians sorted out which texts belonged in their closed canon and what those texts meant. In the third century, for example, Origen argued for the divine origins of the law of Moses on the basis that it had, unlike any other known law code, commended itself to citizens of many nations and cultures, who would submit even to persecution in order to uphold its precepts.[2] He goes on to insist on the impossibility of proving their inspiration (*theopneustos* again) prior to the "sojourning" of Jesus Christ in the world.[3] That view raises certain problems, but it speaks to the high Christocentrism of the ancient Christian understanding of the Old and New Testaments.

This sort of explanation must challenge a modern audience conditioned by the Enlightenment's skepticism and fairly narrow understanding of how beliefs are formed or truth discerned. After all, the argument from international acceptance would also count in favor of Islam and Muhammed's revelation. More pertinently to Origen's own era, it would count for the contemporary justifications of Roman rule, which had gained wide acceptance in his era.

However, his argument is not really an abstract one: he does not ask, Of all the possible religious and non-religious options most plausible to an observer who knew nothing about any of them in advance, which would be most convincing? That sort of mental experiment, so characteristic of our own age, would not have made much sense in his era. Nor does it really account for much in ours. His argument is ex post facto. What is it about the faith we have received as a gift that makes sense?

Rowan Williams points to the need for trust in our everyday lives, particularly in an era when we assume by default that the system is rigged against us and that our neighbor is not to be trusted. The core instinct of Christian faith is to trust "Jesus to be working for [the believer], not for

2. Origen, *On First Principles*, 4.1.1–2. For a critical edition and translation of the text, see Origen, *On First Principles*, ed. and trans. John Behr, Oxford Early Christian Texts, 2 vols. (Oxford: Oxford University Press, 2017).

3. Origen, *On First Principles*, 4.1.6.

any selfish goals" and to believe "that what [the believer] sees and hears when Jesus is around is the truth."[4] Trust is in a person, not an abstract, falsifiable proposition. That person is God and, Christians believe, God manifest in Jesus Christ. (Christian theology enjoys, therefore, both points of convergence and divergence with Judaism or Islam.)

In a world in which social media has made us antisocial and instant communication has made listening hard, trust often eludes us, especially trust in God. As Williams points out, however, the God of the Bible is not one thing among others, nor is God dependent on us for anything. The divine outreach to us comes as pure grace, undeserved favor, completely independent of our merits, no matter how great they may be. This claim does not take us down the road of hyper-Calvinism in which our evil is the only notable thing about us. Quite the opposite, it argues that God's love for the good includes us in its scope and consequences.

For some strands of Christian theology, it has not been enough to anchor a notion of the Bible in Christology or a notion of divine love. So threatening has the Enlightenment critique of religion seemed, that some theologians, no doubt motivated by the most honorable of intentions, have tried to secure their spiritual flanks by arguing that the precise words of the biblical text come from God. Sometimes a very fine distinction between mechanical dictation and verbal plenary inspiration is made (though it is not easy to spot the real difference). Probably the most eloquent and learned exponent of such a view was Benjamin B. Warfield, the last major exponent of the Princeton theology.

Warfield insists that the words of the prophets were precisely and only those given by God, apart from any choice or personality trait by the prophets themselves. He writes, "The marks of the several individualities imprinted on the messages of the prophets, in other words, are only part of the general fact that these messages are couched in human language, and in no way beyond that general fact affect their purity as direct communications from God."[5] That view is understandable as a reaction against late nineteenth-century biblical scholarship

4. Rowan Williams, *Tokens of Trust: An Introduction to Christian Belief* (Louisville: Westminster John Knox, 2007), 5.

5. Benjamin Breckenridge Warfield, *The Inspiration and Authority of the Bible*, ed. Samuel G. Craig and Cornelius van Til (1948; reprint ed.; Philadelphia: Presbyterian and Reformed, 1967), 94.

that understood the prophets as large souls with vivid imaginations, whose spiritual insights exceeded those of most human beings. That is, Warfield and the emerging fundamentalism of the late nineteenth and early twentieth century countered a highly romantic notion of the evolution of religion with one that minimized the human dimensions of the biblical text almost to the vanishing point, quite without any support in the texts themselves.

Nineteenth-century liberal theology seems impossibly quaint today, as does Warfield's theological formalism. Most Christians have not adopted his approach, of course, though it does have wide currency among millions of evangelicals and fundamentalists around the world. It is hardly a marginal position. At the same time, most theologians have not tried to nail down the ins and outs of inspiration and authority, leaving what we believe to be a healthy vagueness, present also in the Patristic and medieval texts. A theology that starts from anxiety, as Warfield's clearly does, can only lead us down blind alleys.

We are opting, then, for something more ecumenical and open-ended. We think we stand in good company. Just to take a highly influential example, the *Catechism of the Roman Catholic Church* insists that "in the condescension of his goodness God speaks to [humankind] in human words," that "through the words of Sacred Scripture, God speaks only one single Word, his one Utterance in whom he expresses himself completely," and that "for this reason, the Church has always venerated the Scriptures as she venerates the Lord's Body."[6] That is, the Bible points inexorably to the divine Word, Jesus Christ, and deserves the same sort of respect the church gives its Lord. The *Catechism* does not insist on a particular theory of how the words of the Bible come from God, leaving at least some openness on ways and means but locating Scripture's authority in the authority of Jesus Christ himself, and thus subjecting interpretation of it to the judgment of the church.[7] Even Protestants (like us) who retain a healthy distrust of church authorities and the potential abuse of power, can sign up to such a view at least as a starting point for reflection on how the biblical texts and the church reading them intersect.

---

6. *Catechism of the Roman Catholic Church*, 2nd ed. (Rome: Libreria Editrice Vaticana, 2019), 101–3.

7. *Catechism of the Roman Catholic Church*, 115–19.

The Taught Book

Most of these reflections by centuries of Christian teachers about the origins and use of the Bible arose in the context of a much larger set of spiritual practices accompanying and conditioning the reading of the Bible. This ecology of learning has developed over the centuries, not always in an upward arc, but often in ways that offer important lessons for us today.

During its first two or three centuries, early Christianity attracted a small minority of subjects of the Roman Empire, and because of that minority status, because of the intellectual life inherited from Judaism, and because of the life-embracing nature of the gospel itself, the followers of Jesus placed a high premium on literacy, careful thought, and learning. The writings of the New Testament served such a role, at least for those already inducted into the faith.

Some writers of New Testament books created a semitechnical term of the Greek verb *katēchein* ("to resound, to speak in the ear"). It became a term for instruction in the faith and the root of the English loanword "catechesis." Luke-Acts speaks of Luke's patron Theophilus and the eloquent teacher of Scripture Apollos being "catechized" (Luke 1:4; Acts 18:25).[8] Paul uses the verb in this same sense as a term of art for instruction in a body of religious knowledge (Rom 2:18 for Torah instruction; 1 Cor 14:19 for illuminating the mind in the gospel; and Gal 6:6). The Galatians usage is particularly revealing inasmuch as the "one catechized" (*ho katēchoumenos*), the person instructed in the faith, enters into a mutually beneficial relationship with the teacher. The teacher/student relationship takes catechism beyond formal practices of instruction into informal, sustained lives of mentorship.

There are many gaps in our knowledge of the earliest church's educational and formational practices. The Pauline model depended so heavily on the personality of the apostle and his associates that it is unlikely to have been replicable outside their orbit, but we simply do not know. A very early church order like Didache (ca. 100 CE) or the letter of Clement to the Corinthians (also late first century) shows a strong interest in reasoned instruction of people already Christians. It is

---

8. The verb is used in the more general Greek sense of "informed" in Acts 21:21, however.

difficult to identify a sharp distinction between postulant (one inquiring seriously about becoming a Christian) and baptized (the one already a Christian). Learning continued in response to the needs and abilities of the individuals in question.

For the first half millennium of Christian history, religious instruction, at least in the major urban centers where the evidence has survived best, often involved a full panoply of formational opportunities. These opportunities included the church's life of prayer and teaching of Scripture and the proclamation of the core doctrines of the church.

A good example is the work of Origen (ca. 185–254 CE) in Alexandria and then Caesarea. Origen worked as a scholar and teacher of multiple audiences, producing both highly technical works like the Hexapla and many homilies and commentaries, probably written for groups possessing varying levels of knowledge. In adopting that multipronged approach, he became a prototype of many other theologians since. Other examples might include the *Apostolic Tradition* attributed to Origen's near contemporary, Hippolytus of Rome, or the earlier works of Justin Martyr, who ran a philosophical school, or Irenaeus bishop of Lyon in Gaul. These texts attempted to explain Christian teaching and living to audiences seeking understanding, or in some cases to defend the faith from its critics or even persecutors.[9]

Without trying to exaggerate the educational achievements of Christians during the first few centuries or assuming a level of consistency that almost certainly did not exist, we could still learn about and perhaps emulate valuable practices. In particular, we might recover the wholesome synthesis of liturgy and intellect, of worship and inquiry. A more holistic approach to reading the Bible in community would be salutary.

A fascinating example of early Christian practice, albeit after the watershed event of Constantine's legalization of Christianity, appears in St. Augustine's so-called *First Catechetical Instruction*, basically an open letter to his friend Deogratias about how to be a good catechist. Augustine calms his friend's nerves about inadequate teaching—surely a feeling every good teacher faces on occasion—and advises him to understand what experiences, and especially what reading and philosophical

---

9. A good summary of the history of early Christian instruction in the faith appears in Everett Ferguson, *The Early Church at Work and Worship*, vol. 2: *Catechesis, Baptism, Eschatology and Martyrdom* (Cambridge: Lutterworth/James Clarke, 2014), 18–51.

reflection, have led the searcher to him as a teacher. Augustine counsels him to interact with the books an educated catechumen has read in order to ensure that the inquirer grasps the Christian understanding of divine love and mercy and avoids heresy. That is, the teacher need not follow a rigid course of instruction but should tailor the lessons to the needs of the student.

Among other topics, Augustine faces head-on the abiding problem of squaring the plain sense of biblical texts with Christian morality and theology. He counsels Deogratias to instruct the learner

> whatsoever he hears from the canonical books that he cannot refer to the love of eternity, and truth, and holiness, and to the love of his neighbor, he may believe to have been said or done with a figurative meaning and endeavor so to understand it to refer to that two-fold [*sic*] love.[10]

That is, Augustine and his readers recognized the challenges of teaching a complex book like the Bible as a theological work, and they sought to address the problems by placing them in a larger intellectual, spiritual, and moral framework.

In the millennium between the collapse of the Western Roman Empire and the Protestant Reformation, religious instruction took many forms. While that period was hardly the "Dark Ages" early modern critics of Christianity chose to call it, it was a period of lower literacy and lower urbanism at least in some areas. The catechesis of an increasingly Christian population was undoubtedly uneven. It often consisted of an explanation of baptism, the Our Father in the vernacular, other prayers, and sometimes the twin commands to love God and neighbor. Texts like the Old High German *Weissenburg Catechism* (just prior to 800 CE) also contained lists of cardinal sins and important prayers. Late medieval instruction added other materials, often varying according to the ideas of local bishops or catechists, and of course in major intellectual centers, the level of learning could be very high indeed. But nothing like a church-wide program existed, or could have existed given the economic

---

10. St. Augustine, *The First Catechetical Instruction (De Catechizandis Rudibus)*, trans. Joseph P. Christopher, Ancient Christian Writers 2 (Westminster, MD: Newman, 1962), 26.50.

and political realities of the era.[11] The idea that catechesis should be localized and fit the needs of individual seekers remains the practice of much of the US branches of the Orthodox Church even today.[12]

Much of that improvisational approach changed during the Reformation of the sixteenth century. The emerging Protestant movement, aided by the new technology of printing, produced a vast array of educational materials, from Martin Luther's two catechisms and Bible translation, to hymnals, prayer books, commentaries, and the full range of genres now familiar to many Christians. Catholics, partly in self-defense, responded in kind. William Tyndale's wish for "the boy that driveth the plough" to know more about Scripture than clerics had in previous generations became a real possibility.[13] Other sorts of learning, some inimical to Tyndale's vision of Christian wholeness, also became just as possible, though that is a different story.

Skipping several centuries, two other phenomena deserve mention because both have exerted huge influences on the life of the church. In Protestant circles, the Sunday school movement began in the late eighteenth century as a way of educating children in factories. The curriculum taught basic literacy and numeracy, as well as religion. That attempt to help working-class children has persisted in some corners of the Protestant Sunday school, though in many others it has lost that aspect as it became a more middle-class phenomenon. As the Sunday school evolved in the nineteenth and twentieth centuries, it often took on other dimensions, including amateur athletics, music-making, and various social and recreational activities. In other words, at least in some settings, the Sunday school appealed more comprehensively to the needs of children and their families than the label "school" seems to imply. The resources available determined the quality of services on

11. A good, if brief, summary with bibliography appears in Hans-Jürgen Fraas, "Catechesis and Catechetics: 2. Middle Ages and Reformation," *Religion Past and Present* 2 (2007): 419–20.

12. Amy Slagle, *The Eastern Church in the Spiritual Marketplace: American Conversions to Orthodox Christianity* (Ithaca, NY: Cornell University Press, 2011), 61–83.

13. John Foxe, *Actes and Monuments of These Latter and Perillous Days, Touching Matters of the Church* (London: John Day, 1563), 570, https://web.archive.org/web/20151017204547/http://www.johnfoxe.org/index.php?realm=text&edition=1563&pageid=570&gototype=modern.

offer, but the aspirations of churches tended to follow the lead of the larger and more affluent ones.[14]

The other development in North America (and elsewhere) was the spread of Roman Catholic alternatives to Protestant education in the public school and the Sunday school movement. The Confraternity of Christian Doctrine (CCD) began in the sixteenth century, but its regular work of the formation of children and adult postulants began in the United States mostly in the nineteenth and twentieth centuries. Often positioning itself against what Martin Marty called "the Puritan spirit," Roman Catholics have linked catechesis to confirmation and the celebration of the Eucharist.[15] After the Second Vatican Council, the Catholic Church in the United States saw renewed attention to catechesis as more dynamic understandings of revelation and Christian life came to the fore, influenced by the important work of Gabriel Moran and others.[16] The doctrinal and moral instruction aimed at children who have received baptism as infants or at adult seekers leads, at least in theory, to a life of regular confession, absolution, and celebration. Connected to CCD and designed explicitly to support it, the Catholic Biblical Association brings to bear the best of biblical scholarship for audiences interested in studying it.

Over the past few decades, Christian religious education has, in many cases, embraced an ecumenical stance that draws on psychology and sociology as well as theology. Forty years ago, a group of scholars led by Jack Seymour and Donald Miller spoke of religious education as instruction, enculturation/socialization, spiritual development,

---

14. On the history of the Sunday school in the United Kingdom, see the essays in Stephen Orchard and John H. Y. Briggs, eds., *The Sunday School Movement: Studies in the Growth and Decline of Sunday Schools* (Eugene, OR: Wipf & Stock, 2007). Many of the developments in the United Kingdom also occurred in the United States, though often on a larger scale, since the British Nonconformist churches were the establishment in the United States. For the United States, see Robert W. Lynn and Elliott Wright, *The Big Little School: 200 Years of the Sunday School*, 2nd ed. (Nashville: Abingdon, 1980).

15. See, e.g., Martin Marty, *Modern American Religion*, vol. 2: *The Noise of Conflict, 1919–1941* (Chicago: University of Chicago Press, 1991), 145–54.

16. Gabriel Moran, *Theology of Revelation* (New York: Herder & Herder, 1966); idem, *Theology of Catechesis* (New York: Herder & Herder, 1966). For a history of this revitalization, see Anne Marie Mongoven, *The Prophetic Spirit of Catechesis: How We Share the Fire in Our Hearts* (New York: Paulist, 2000), esp. 1–86.

liberation, and interpretation. They sought a multidimensional approach.[17] Similarly, Mary Elizabeth Mullino Moore explicitly explored methodology in teaching with approaches such as case teaching, Gestalt, phenomenological methods, narrative, and conscientization, all forms of transformational teaching and learning.[18] And James Michael Lee, a prominent Roman Catholic religious educator, spoke at the cusp of the third millennium of a prophetic mode of religious instruction that took both the noun and adjective seriously.[19] More recently still, Beverly Johnson-Miller and Robert Pazmiño called for an interest in educational foundations as a way of supporting "the quest for a radical Christianity that returns to the spiritual and theological roots evident in the life and ministry of Jesus Christ."[20]

Another helpful approach comes from Richard Osmer, who draws on the apostle Paul's threefold approach to formation as catechesis, exhortation, and discernment. Osmer's work influences much of our thinking throughout this book. He overlays the ancient model, which has persisted in the church's life in various forms for almost two millennia, with his own frames. They focus on practices, curriculum, leadership, and pilgrimage.[21] This fourfold model takes seriously a congregation's situation in its local environment, its history, and the ways it forms itself through liturgy, mutual service, and connections to the problems of its world.

Osmer's last item, pilgrimage, owes much to Thomas Groome while it also adds an important dimension to traditional reflections on the church's life. Osmer thinks of the church as a community in which individuals explore their personal vocations from God at their own pace, in response to whatever life brings. The freedom to be on pilgrimage

---

17. Jack L. Seymour and Donald E. Miller, eds., *Contemporary Approaches to Christian Education* (Nashville: Abingdon, 1982).

18. Mary Elizabeth Mullino Moore, *Teaching from the Heart: Theology and Educational Method* (Harrisburg, PA: Trinity Press International, 1998).

19. James Michael Lee, "Vision, Prophecy, and Forging the Future," in *Forging a Better Religious Education in the Third Millennium*, ed. James Michael Lee (Birmingham, AL: Religious Education Press, 2000), 243–67.

20. Beverly Johnson-Miller and Robert Pazmiño, "Christian Education Foundations: Retrospects and Prospects," *Christian Education Journal* 17 (2020): 560 (560–76).

21. Richard Robert Osmer, *The Teaching Ministry of Congregations* (Louisville: Westminster John Knox, 2005), 63.

together marks the healthy church. He understands this aspect of the church's life in terms of individualization theory as it plays out in contemporary societies. As he puts it, "In a differentiated society of segmented roles, more freedom and responsibility falls [*sic*] on individuals and nuclear families to knit together a meaningful pattern across the different spheres of life and across the life cycle."[22] Piecing together one's calling over a lifetime will be a highly individualized process, but it also occurs in a community of persons who help each other do that vocational work. The formation of a Christian self-understanding requires open-ended processes of interaction that allow at least some un-predetermined outcomes.

Osmer's call to listen deeply to a given context rather than falling back on generalizations (positive or negative) makes an important point. The church's formational enterprise cannot be merely reactive. Our story is not merely a counter-story. Our rituals exclude some other alternative rituals, but do not draw their meaning from the opposition alone. Our critique of our own lives and those celebrated by other narratives must remain ethically rich and humane. Our pursuit of wisdom requires a rigorous honesty, as well as a pedagogy of joy. All of that can emerge from a process of reading ourselves within larger contexts.

In this brief survey, we have not aimed at anything remotely like comprehensiveness. Done well, tracing the history of education in Christian Scripture as part of an ecology of learning would require multiple specialists filling several volumes. We only wish to make two more modest points:

- There has never been a time in the past when the teaching of Scripture inducted everyone fully into a wise, careful understanding of the texts and their implications for life;
- Nevertheless, an extraordinary level of creativity, pastoral care, and intellectual comprehensiveness has existed, allowing the church to survive for two thousand years as a recognizable body, despite its many divisions along regional, liturgical, and theological lines.

22. Osmer, *Teaching Ministry*, 180.

The paradox of Christian unity and diversity (often rivalry) has operated in the realm of Bible study as much as everywhere else. Playing to the possibilities of unity rather than division can lead to the renewal of the church in communities, congregations, and families. There is a lot to play for.

On Taught Text

When we speak with pastors and church members, as we do almost every day, we hear anxiety and confusion, as well as chastened hope. The global pandemic exposed much of the fragility of many congregations, just as it also opened up possibilities for reimagining congregational life. Pastors faced the practical challenges of distributing the Eucharist and providing pastoral care for a newly isolated population.

The church in the United States (and no doubt elsewhere) has just begun to sort through its current reality. It must face down the heresy of Christian nationalism and white supremacy. It must respond to criticisms of its ethics, both to the ideas and the practices. The cracks that have emerged over the past few decades have become wide enough that large chunks of the edifice have slipped off altogether. Yet such moments of sickness and death also open the door to resurrection. There can be no resurrection without death. That is surely a given for anyone thinking in a Christian way.

The brief history of teaching Scripture shows that the church has repeatedly reinvented its understanding of religious formation and the Bible's part in it. Many elements have remained constant, but adaptability and creativity have frequently flourished. There is ample precedent for the hope that, once again, renewal may occur, probably in many forms.

The key to the renewal of the teaching of Scripture lies in the nature of the texts themselves. At this point, then, we turn to the modalities of Scripture: narrative, ritual, prophecy, and wisdom. We use the term "mode" advisedly, though we remain open to other expressions. The point is that the literary genres or clusters of genres that make up the Old and New Testaments do work in the communities reading them. The church reads these books because it needs to do so. Or put another way, these books help the church do its spiritual work as a story-making community that engages in ritual (worships), critiques and reimagines its own life and the life of the world, and cultivates wisdom. The fit between text and life is real, even if it must be renegotiated again and again. That fit is the subject of the next four chapters.

As Karl Barth (and possibly Charlotte von Kirschbaum) put it, "apart from Jesus Christ Himself there is still this other form of the Word of God, which Scripture needs to be the Word of God, just as it needs Scripture. Preaching and the sacrament of the Church do indeed need the basis and authority and authenticity of the original Word of God in Scripture to be the Word of God. But Scripture also needs proclamation by preaching and sacrament."[23] We get to enjoy the dance of two lifelong, if not always harmonious, partners, the Bible and the church.

23. Karl Barth, *Church Dogmatics*, vol. 1, part 2: *The Doctrine of the Word of God, Part 2*, trans. G. W. Bromiley (Edinburgh: T&T Clark, 1963).

CHAPTER 3

The Biblical Story and the Power of Storytelling in Context

In the beginning was the story.

Archaeologists tell us that thousands of years ago on the Great Plains, hunter-gatherers assembled every year for great bison kills.[1] They cooperated in herding the giant beasts into ravines where they could kill some with their spears and share the meat in days of feasting. How did they know to travel hundreds of miles to the feast? Surely they told stories of the previous years' hunts. That capacity, and not just their trade in material objects like flint for tools, allowed them to fashion a society without governments, buildings, means of mass communication, or even settled homes.

That capacity for, and love of, story certainly defines us as human beings. And it pervades much of our lives. Humans are natural storytellers, and we have been honing the art for millennia. But storytelling is more than just a pleasant amusement. It can save lives, which is why some people wear medical alert bracelets. They tell a story of pathology and need. It can also kill, as the twentieth century's gigantic storytelling exercises about, pick them, Jews, Christians, Communists, capitalists, foreigners, Black people, White people, and just about any other group you can name, show all too well. Storytelling in the wrong hands can be dangerous. In the right hands, it can build worlds.

Yes, there are entire organizations dedicated to the art of storytelling: news media outlets, history classes, stand-up comedy clubs, theaters for plays or musicals, and above all, religious communities. Families

---

1. Leland C. Bement, Brian J. Carter, PollyAnna Jelley, Kristen Carlson, and Scott Fine, "Badger Hole: Towards Defining a Folsom Bison Hunting Complex along the Beaver River, Oklahoma," *Plains Anthropologist* 57/221 (2012): 53–62.

around the kitchen table tell of the past and induct their children into a line of succession. All of these institutions of human civilization trade in story. The stories may be trivial or grand, ancient or up-to-the-minute, describing universal human behaviors or incomprehensibly particular ones. Yet in every case, they share in common four elements that bear on our exploration here: the storyteller or bard; the performance itself, with its prior rules for making the story engaging; the story itself with its plot, characters, and problems to solve; and the audience, who must care about the story at least a little. These elements constitute the event of storytelling. They must all coalesce for the story to work, that is, for the audience to hang with it and reflect upon it as a vehicle for advancing their own understanding of life.

In the present discussion, we are interested in a particular set of stories, those of the Bible, and a particular location for their telling, the church. We will argue that the performance of the biblical story can be understood not only for the ancient world but for our own, and that we can learn from the biblical texts' own storytelling practices how to retell it in our own day. In retelling, the ancient story comes to include new characters and new plotlines as the church interrogates it, performs and celebrates it, and invites its members and friends into the narrative itself. The mechanical repetition of the ancient story's words does not suffice when what is required is a living community seeking meaning within it.

Our argument proceeds in several steps: a brief description of the approach to story in the Bible, an account of the plotline of the biblical story, and a set of proposals for creating an ecology of storytelling in the church's life. This movement recognizes that telling the biblical story, or rather always retelling it, creates a dynamic in which the listening and telling community reorients itself as a group of people living inside God's story through the story of their own baptism and its outworking in their lives.

The Art of Storytelling and Making Meaning

When we turn from stories in general to the biblical story in particular, we find ourselves immediately in a world of intricate and intimate discussions. In the ancient Near East and eastern Mediterranean, storytelling took place in several settings, especially those associated with religious events. Bards recited sometimes lengthy stories that ran to thousands of lines, regaling audiences with tales of ancient heroes and villains, whether Gilgamesh and Huwawa or Achilles and Hector or Odysseus and his wife's luckless suitors. Many of these stories migrated from culture to culture. So, for example, themes of heroic kingship that began in Mesopotamia, probably in the third millennium BCE or even earlier, migrated to the Hittite Empire and Mitanni, and from there to Syria-Palestine to the south and Greece to the west. This is why similar themes appear in both ancient Near Eastern and Greek tales, from Gilgamesh to the *Iliad*. It is not simply a question of folklore taking the same forms in different settings, but of real influence across languages and cultures.[2]

These tales were told by professional storytellers, long practiced in the substance of the story and the art of its performance in words and music. Most of these singers of tales remain anonymous. Even traditions that finally give names to these singers of tales, such as the Greek singers Hesiod and Homer, usually keep other names in the background. The story belongs in some sense to the community as a whole.

In the Bible itself, the storytellers behind the text remain completely anonymous, whether we mean the writers of most narrative texts or the storytellers behind those writers. We have no direct access to the oral traditions, though it would be fairly silly to deny their existence. We do have written texts, which, however, show all the signs of orality, as they were written more for the ear than for the eye (much as plays or songs still are). As Robert Kawashima has argued, the texts we have exist at some remove from the oral tradition and show signs of literary inventiveness,[3] but even so, the creators of these texts did not presuppose an audience of individuals silently reading. The texts had a public face from the beginning and the size and diversity of the audience have only grown over time. Just as no archaeologist would assume that the foundations surviving in the trench were the only part of the house that ever existed, readers of the Bible should recognize that the written

---

2. For a very thorough study of these issues, see Mary R. Bachvarova, *From Hittite to Homer: The Anatolian Background of Ancient Greek Epic* (Cambridge: Cambridge University Press, 2016).

3. Robert S. Kawashima, *Biblical Narrative and the Death of the Rhapsode* (Bloomington: Indiana University Press, 2004).

texts we have were part of a much larger storytelling edifice, which now survives only in fragments.

Yet even those fragments hide some of themselves, revealing their creators only sporadically. We do not know who wrote Joshua–Kings (the so-called Deuteronomistic History) or the books of Chronicles or the Four Gospels, for example. With rare exceptions (for example, Luke 1:1–4), even the authors of the books who partially reveal themselves, the storytellers to whom we have the most access, remain far in the background. No biblical narrative work explicitly claims a named individual as an author. Why? And what does this anonymity say about the performance of the text as a story, either in antiquity or in the church today? What does it say about the nature of the story itself?

In the earlier biblical narratives, the practice of anonymity simply carried on the greater ancient Near Eastern tradition of how texts were put forward. But by the time of the New Testament, some authors had long since named themselves in their texts or been named by those reading them at the very least. This is why the Jewish and Christian traditions eventually felt a need to assign names to at least some books (though still not Joshua–Kings or Chronicles). However, the larger sense that this text belongs not to the author but to the readers remained. Anonymity invites the reader of the text into the meaning-making process.

The Bible and Church as Bard

To think through how the Bible tells stories and why that might matter to our understanding of the plot and characterizations of those stories, we should recognize clues in the Bible itself to its performance. These include descriptions of speeches telling the ancient stories (Josh 24; Neh 9) and other recitations placed in the mouths of honored storytellers (Deut 32–33; Ps 78). Other clues are more subtle, as when Second Isaiah merges two major stories on the assumption that the audience will understand what has just happened:

> Up, up, YHWH's arm,
> Up as in olden days,
>   ancient generations—

Aren't you the one that split Rahav,
　　impaled the dragon?
Aren't you the one drying up the Sea,
　　the waters of the Great Abyss,
Making a track among the sea valleys
　　for the redeemed to pass over? (Isa 51:9–10)

That text conflates the story of the world's creation through combat with the forces threatening life,[4] and the crossing of the Reed Sea in the exodus (also after combat with the political forces enslaving human beings), as though they were simply two episodes in one grand story. The reader must understand the connection. The virtuosity of the poet can only work if the audience has been trained to catch at least the basic connections the poet makes. This training does not begin when the audience first encounters the text but earlier in prior textual encounters. The poet draws on stories already known.

At the same time, texts train their readers, by turns deepening, connecting, affirming, or confounding the expectations readers bring to the text based on their own experiences of reading or indeed living. The main narratives of the Old and New Testaments share many features (not least because the New Testament writers of the Gospels and Acts drew on the older canonical texts as their primary model). There are several features that deserve reflection.

Spare storytelling that respects the reader. These features include economy of words. Spare storytelling usually provides only enough detail to make the episode understandable. The audience must know enough about the characters and their actions to make sense of the story but not so much that interpretation is overly determined. So, for example, the storyteller does not explain why God tested Abraham's limits in demanding Isaac as an offering or why David was preferred over his brothers and other rivals or why Jesus chose the twelve men he did as his apostles. The sparsity of details gives readers space to wonder, reflect, and so create meaning. Those hearing the story partner with the teller to allow the characters within it to live. As Erich Auerbach

---

4. Bernard Batto, *Slaying the Dragon: Mythmaking in the Biblical Tradition* (Louisville: Westminster John Knox, 1992).

put it in his classic work *Mimesis*, the speech of biblical characters "serves to indicate thoughts which remain unexpressed."[5] Economy of detail bespeaks the view of many biblical authors that much of human experience remains opaque, even to ourselves. The self-exposing, self-glorifying speech of the hero, the tiny minority of humanity, gives way to the silences of humanity as a whole.

This openness of the biblical text requires communities reading it to practice several virtues. Andrew P. Rogers identifies them as honesty and faithfulness in handling the church's tradition, humility and confidence in dealing with what the community of readers knows, and faithfulness and openness in mediating the faith to others.[6] All of those virtues come into play in reading biblical narrative in the church, precisely because the stories from Genesis to Revelation are open to multiple interpretations, not all of them constructive, ethical, or spiritually enlightened.

Non-omniscience. For modern readers, the biblical stories' economy of words and open-endedness become most bothersome when the narrator refuses to reveal the emotional state of the characters. Because the narrators are not omniscient, they do not provide direct access to the inner state of the characters. Put more precisely, the ancient narrators do not share the modern conception of the person as primarily an inner state only opaquely perceivable to the outside. They also put much less stock in self-revelation through talking than we tend to do.

An instructive case might be the story of Joseph's self-revelation to his brothers. After Joseph, in his guise of the intimidating Egyptian high official, threatens Benjamin with imprisonment, Judah offers himself as a hostage in his baby brother's place. The story redeems Judah, to some extent, for his previous failure to protect Joseph or regard his own father's grief at the death of a favored son (Gen 44:18–34). Judah has learned honor and perhaps even empathy, and he can express as much by offering himself as a substitute for Benjamin.

5. Erich Auerbach, *Mimesis: The Representation of Reality in Western Literature*, trans. Willard R. Trask, introduction by Edward W. Said (1953; Princeton: Princeton University Press, 2003), 11.

6. Andrew P. Rogers, *Congregational Hermeneutics: How Do We Read?* (Burlington, VT: Ashgate, 2015), 24 and throughout.

By the time the Joseph narrative reaches this scene in Egypt, new possibilities for Jacob's whole family have emerged. At precisely this point, then, unable to contain himself any longer, Joseph dismisses his Egyptian staff so he can speak to the Hebrew grain buyers alone. The story does not directly reveal Joseph's inner thoughts but does say,

> He gave his voice over to weeping, which the Egyptians and even the entire house of Pharaoh heard. Then Joseph said to his brothers, "I am Joseph. Is my father still alive?" But his brothers could not answer him for they were horrified before him. (Gen 45:2–3)

Joseph's understandable resolve to toy with his brothers' feelings has collapsed under the weight of Judah's willingness to sacrifice himself for his brother. And all of this is expressed with the single word "weeping." Conversely, the brothers' reaction might involve a complex stew of emotions—astonishment, fear, guilt, confusion—which the narrator sums up in one word, "horrified." The best news possible does not seem such initially. Yet the reader can see none of this emotional, interior state of the various characters except through the extraordinary economy of contrasting Joseph's noisiness with the brothers' stunned silence.

This example does not merely illustrate the brilliance of some biblical storytellers, though it does that. It also shows how complexity of human emotion can come through. Readers may discuss the emotional complexity of all the characters in the story, the clash between the ethical demands of the situation and any latent feelings of shame or desire for revenge, or the intersections of power and vulnerability. The story becomes a site for serious theological and moral reflection.

The narrator's self-obscuration. The hiding of the interior person continues for the narrators themselves. Part of the biblical narrator's method of storytelling involves hiding the existence of the narrator. Peter Machinist has rightly described this phenomenon as a means of writing "history." He describes ancient practices of presenting the narrator as the "absent-I" (which fits most biblical storytelling), the "pseudo-I" (in which the author creates a persona telling the story, as with royal inscriptions set forth in the name of the king), and the "autobiographical-I" (in which the author actually represents his or her own story, as in part of Nehemiah). As he notes, these various styles of

presentation "are all vehicles for communicating authority: the authority of human rulership, of pre-existing tradition . . . and, finally, of the
divine as the basic force in controlling history."[7]

The biblical texts do not, by and large, underwrite political authority,
either of the kings of Israel and Judah or of foreign powers occupying
the Israelite homeland. They often expose and resist or even counteract such power. However, they also hold up other kinds of authority,
including the authority of the traditional stories of divine redemption
and sustenance of the world. They represent Israel's God as not only
the companion along the way for migrating people (Gen 46:4), but as
the ruler of the universe (Isa 40–55) whose plans of redemption surpass
human comprehension (Isa 55:10–11).

In his reflection on the meaning of the cross in a world of violence
against Black and Brown people, James Cone says that Christians need
"the imagination to relate the message of the cross to one's own social
reality."[8] For White Christians, that means coming to see Christ in
the lynched bodies of Black people, and for those oppressed, it means
coming to love themselves in spite of the hate directed toward them.
That sort of radical critique of a domesticated gospel, which Cone rightly
finds in much of the church in the United States, draws on the deepest
instincts of the biblical texts themselves. Even when they seek to support
a given social or theological program, they contain within themselves
the seeds of other points of view.

Nor is this potential creativity limited to the overtly narrative texts
like 2 Kings or Matthew. Machinist's insightful treatment of the narrator
in historical texts can be extended further into the biblical witness, to
other forms of narratives, including the book of Psalms. Many psalms,
especially those of lament, highlight the pseudo-I, the narrator who
seems to be one person but is really a character into whom all those
performing the psalm can pour their own complex identity. They may
do so in the context of the larger story of Israel, contrasting their own

---

7. Peter Machinist, "The Voice of the Historian in the Ancient Mediterranean and
Near Eastern World," *Int* 57 (2003): 127 (117–37). We bracket here questions of verifi-
ability and historical reliability of these texts. Our word "story" limns a broader category
of narratives than Machinist's "history." Still, his insights into one subset of narratives
elucidate other categories as well.

8. James Cone, *The Cross and the Lynching Tree* (Maryknoll, NY: Orbis, 2017), 158.

experience of suffering with the story's implicit promise of recurring salvation. So, for example, Ps 44 can insist that

> O Elohim, we have heard with our own ears
>   what our ancestors told us,
> How you did marvelous things in their days,
>   in days of old. (Ps 44:1[2])[9]

and then insist that the singer had not trusted his own military might but solely in God. Nevertheless, the storyteller claims,

> You have rejected us and humiliated us,
>   not going out with our armies. (v. 9[10])

That is, the story—and psalms of lament are stories—explores the role of the "I" in the context of a larger story. The story of the lament unfolds in such a way that many persons can enter it (and have done so for more than two millennia). By obscuring the narrator, the text creates a kind of objectivity in the story, a sense of its inevitability that the audience must work hard to challenge.

Stories and the story. These elements of storytelling technique give some indication of the skill behind the biblical texts, as well as of the sheer delight in good storytelling that seems at times to take over. Despite their appearance of detachment from the characters whose lives they portray, there is no reason to read these texts as dry matter-of-fact reporting of events, nor to distill from them at every turn some powerful spiritual meaning. Rather, the reader wrestles with the text in order to discover what it might mean.

Yet the biblical texts are part of a larger story that spans millennia and defines the core identity of the people celebrating that story. The effort at summarizing that story in manageable form appears early and often in the Bible. One early version occurs in Deuteronomy 26, the conclusion of the law collection at the core of the book. As part of a ritual around the offering of the first fruits, the worshiper is to say,

---

9. Where the English and Hebrew versification differs, the English is given first followed by the Hebrew.

> My ancestor was a perishing Aramean, and he went down to Egypt and lived there as a small migrant community but became there a great and numerous nation. But the Egyptians ill-treated us and oppressed us and forced hard labor on us. We cried to YHWH our ancestors' God, and YHWH heard our cry and saw our oppression and our toil and our torment. So YHWH brought us from Egypt with a strong hand and extended arm and with a great miracle and signs and wonders. Then he brought us to this place and gave us this land, a land flowing with milk and honey. Therefore, I am now bringing the first fruit of the ground that YHWH gave me. (Deut 26:5–10)

It would be interesting to know the extent to which Deuteronomy innovated this ritual. It has the ring of a family religion practice that Deuteronomy, in its efforts to centralize worship at the temple, has taken over and modified.[10] But the prehistory of the text is unfortunately no longer accessible. What is clear is that the story the worshiper recites summarizes Deuteronomy's understanding of Israel's key experience, the descent to Egypt, the deliverance from slavery, and the grant of the promised land. The book calls upon adults to recite this story at least once a year, cementing its key elements of dependence, deliverance, and gratitude into the superstructure of every family's life.

That process of summarizing story appears in numerous Old Testament texts of varying genres, as well as in the New Testament. For example, Paul can remind the Corinthians not only of the deliverance at the Red Sea and the wilderness wanderings (1 Cor 10:1–13), but of the Christ story, transmitted from one tradition bearer to another, of how Jesus died, was buried, and arose, "according to the Scriptures" (1 Cor 15:1–8). That is, Jesus's life formed a plot point, indeed for Christians the climax, of a much longer story.

It is probably anachronistic to attach the label "creeds" to statements like those in Deuteronomy or 1 Corinthians or even such short narrative summaries as 1 Timothy 3:16's "who was manifest in flesh, justified in spirit, seen by angels, preached to the nations, trusted in the world,

---

10. For the literary issues, see Eckard Otto, *Deuteronomium 12–34*, vol 4: 23,16–34,12, Herder Theologische Kommentar zum Alten Testament (Freiburg: Herder, 2017), 1882–85; Jeffrey Tigay, *Deuteronomy*, Jewish Publication Society Torah Commentary (Philadelphia: JPS, 1996), 240–42.

received up into glory." These texts and others summarize the story's key plot points for educational purposes, allowing the audience of the story to navigate its many twists and turns and to perform it in their own lives as they imitate its key characters. The question remains, however, what is the shape of that story, and why does that matter?

The Plotline

In recounting the story that the Bible tells, it should be obvious that any summary is contestable, as is the interpretation of given episodes. The meaning does not lie entirely in the text itself, but in the ongoing interaction of the text with the community of readers. Most biblical writers, because they were good storytellers, avoided over-determining the meaning of an episode or its relationships to others in the same sequence. In other words, the summaries within various biblical texts remain subject to negotiation and reexamination.

At the same time, however, the act of negotiating meaning presupposes the ability to reach some sort of agreement with others, however provisional. It would be silly to imagine the daughters of Zelophehad to be as important characters as Moses's sister Miriam or the various Miriams/Marys of the New Testament, or to think the crossing of the Red Sea only slightly outweighs in importance the story of Gideon's men lapping up water like dogs. Some episodes have implications for the flow of the narrative far more than others. In other words, common sense in reading, while not an infallible guide, helps readers.

Several key plot points influence so many others that they must appear in any summary of the Christian Bible, with most of them also shared with the Jewish Bible. These include

- the creation of the world;
- the call of Abraham, Sarah, and their family, hence the election of Israel;
- the exodus;
- the giving of Torah at Sinai;
- the rise and fall of the monarchy, especially David's;
- the erection, destruction, and rebuilding of the Temple;
- the call of prophets;
- the mass deportations and return;

- the life, death, and resurrection of Jesus;
- the call of disciples into the church; and
- the eschaton.

These elements appear repeatedly in the storytelling of the Christian Bible, often intertwining with each other.

Take, for example, Luke's story of Jesus's failed sermon at Nazareth (Luke 4:16–30). Jesus stood in the synagogue to read, "as was his custom," and turned to Isaiah 61. When he evoked the ancient promise of a renewed Israel, he cited a story with characters and a plotline (the prophet will announce God's freeing of the deported citizens of Judah and Jerusalem). The text he cites figures in a larger story of forced migration, return, and renewal. That basically orienting move won over his audience, for the moment. However, Luke's Jesus turns the tables on himself, as well as his audience, by reminding them of two other stories, the feeding of the widow of Zarephath by Elijah, and the healing of Naaman the Syrian by Elisha. The blunt reminder that part of Israel's story involves Gentiles receiving God's help goes hand in hand with a call to decision: Israel must also be willing to receive divine mercy and so must see itself as needing such. The story ends in a near lynching. It becomes a paradigm not only for the ministry of Jesus, but for the life of the church imitating Jesus (the theme of the book of Acts).

In recounting this story, it is possible for modern Christians to go wrong. One wrong move is to make this a story about the *rejection* of Israel, the common tool of anti-Semites across the political spectrum even to this day. But that move simply inverts Luke's point: all are welcome to God's dispensing of mercy, and each may rejoice at the coming of the others. The long story of Israel is fundamentally a story of God's openness to all human beings. Jesus's reading of the story—or better, Luke's reading of Jesus's reading—opens the promises to all.

This small example, then, illustrates the interlocking, reinforcing nature of the biblical stories. The creators of these works labored creatively within inherited frameworks set by prior narratives and the needs of their audiences.

Filtering. Making a list like this, however, involves decisions about which stories to include or exclude, or in other words, a process of filtering. The process has gone on since the beginning of the formation of the Bible itself, as some stories were developed in different ways for different purposes. To take the most notable example, the exodus story could be a moral touchstone for current behavior in both prophets (Amos 2:10–14) and law (Exod 22:21–24[20–23]), or it could be a model for a new act of divine salvation (Isa 51:10). A key story can stimulate further stories.

Conversely, a story can drop out of the narrative. Many Christians reading the list above will notice the absence of the story of the fall, for example, despite its prominence in many strands of Christian theology, especially those influenced by St. Augustine and his readers during the Reformation. Yet the Old Testament never returns explicitly to the story presented in Genesis 3 and in the New Testament direct influence appears chiefly in the theology of Paul (Rom 5:12–21; 1 Cor 15:21–22; 1 Tim 2:13–15).[11] The earliest tradition made much less of it than was later the case, and its reintroduction has produced highly contentious debates about the nature and extent of human sinfulness.[12] We are dealing, then, not just with the biblical text, but with the filters that communities of readers apply to it.

In a discussion of this process of literary filtering by reading communities over time, the Italian literary critic Umberto Eco made an instructive remark:

11. Cf. Sir 15:12–20 and 17:1–24, both of which explain sin as a human choice since God has not commanded anyone to sin. See the fine discussion of the interpretive afterlife of Gen 2–3 by Gary A. Anderson, *The Genesis of Perfection: Adam and Eve in Jewish and Christian Imagination* (Louisville: Westminster John Knox, 2001); Matthew J. Goff, "Genesis 1–3 and Conceptions of Humankind in 4QInstruction, Philo and Paul," in *Early Christian Literature and Intertextuality*, ed. Craig A. Evans and H. Daniel Zacharias, LNTS 392 (London: T&T Clark, 2009), 2.114–25; Joel Kaminsky, "Paradise Regained," in *Jews, Christians, and the Theology of Hebrew Scriptures*, ed. Alice Bellis and Joel Kaminsky (Atlanta: SBL, 2000), 15–44. On the overall history of the idea of the fall, see Julius Gross, *Geschichte der Erbsündendogmas: Ein Beitrag zur Geschichte des Problem vom Ursprung des Übels*, 4 vols. (Munich: Reinhardt, 1960–1972).

12. There is an enormous amount of literature on the notion of original sin, which we cannot rehearse here. Perhaps it is sufficient to say, as Janice McRandal puts it, "The idea of original sin, when placed within the Christian account of creation and redemption, ensures that creaturely difference is held together in solidarity and not cast into permanent fragmentation." See Janice McRandal, *Christian Doctrine and the Grammar of Difference: A Contribution to Feminist Systematic Theology* (Minneapolis: Fortress, 2015), 82.

Culture filters things, telling us what we should retain and what we must forget. . . . Discussions between people can only take place on the basis of a shared encyclopaedia.[13]

"Encyclopedia" in the lingo of semiotics is the whole network of significations that a culture shares, the whole assemblage of the group's knowledge of the world. An intelligent Martian, if such existed, reading the Bible would come to different conclusions about it than would a Christian, a Jew, or a Muslim because of their different histories. Modern Western readers encountering stories of tensions within polygamous marriages may struggle to think through what justice would look like in such a cultural situation. Urbanites and suburbanites may struggle to understand the dynamics of range management and animal husbandry in some of the Genesis stories, or the nature imagery of the prophets. We see what we are used to seeing.

Moreover, the more readers share ideas and assumptions with each other, the more likely they are to identify both points of agreement and disagreement, while finding fewer areas of mutual incomprehension. An intelligent Martian would probably not enter the debates about the recipients of baptism held between, say, Baptists and Catholics.

This observation may explain some of the signs in the New Testament itself about the search for agreement on the meaning of the overall story. Take the presentations in the Acts of the Apostles, for example. Several decades ago, C. H. Dodd argued that the sermons in Acts reflect the kerygmatic preaching of the earliest church, differing in small details from the developed preaching of Paul. This "primitive preaching" consisted of, among other elements, seven basic points: the fulfillment of prophecy ("according to the Scriptures") in the coming of Jesus as the inaugural event of the new era of human history; Jesus's descent from David; Jesus's death as deliverance from the present age; Jesus's burial; his resurrection; his exaltation, and his return as Judge of all.[14] New Testament scholarship has deepened and nuanced Dodd's presentation, but the basic idea stands. The earliest preaching of Jesus's

13. Umberto Eco and Jean-Claude Carrière, *This Is Not the End of the Book*, ed. Jean-Philippe de Tonnac, trans. Polly McLean (Evanston, IL: Northwestern University Press, 2012), 82.

14. C. H. Dodd, *The Apostolic Preaching and Its Developments* (1935; reprint ed. New York: Harper & Row, 1964), 17.

followers presented a story, deeply rooted in the Old Testament story. Yet this story was not told by rote, but rather developed in different ways for various audiences, not just as a technique of persuasion but as a token of deepening reflection on the story's meaning.

The key phrase here is "according to the Scriptures" (see 1 Cor 15:3). The church repudiated the idea that their story marked a clean break from Israel's story. Jesus's disciples understood him—and he seems to have understood himself—as an heir to the promises to Abraham. In his ongoing life as both the humble Galilean carpenter/teacher and the exalted cosmic Christ, his followers found an embodiment of the promises God had made to the ancestors and perpetually keeps to them and, through them, the world at large. Either/or readings have to go by the wayside. Jesus could fulfill the promises without negating them or foreclosing ever new layers of fulfillment.

Yet the telling of the large story can be filtered in different ways, depending on the encyclopedia shared between teller and audience. For example, the sermon attributed to St. Stephen the Protomartyr recounts the story of the ancestors. "The God of Glory," it begins, "appeared to our ancestor Abraham" (Acts 7:2). It goes on to recite well-known stories of his sojourning first in Harran and then in Canaan, the birth of Isaac, the trip of the ancestors to Egypt, their suffering back in the promised land, the travails of Moses, the exodus and wilderness wanderings, and the work of David and Solomon. The sermon alters the sequence of events at strategic points, but in ways that an audience familiar with Genesis and Exodus would find intelligible and plausible. A shared encyclopedia again.

Stephen's portrayal of the Moses story is striking. With other Second Temple–period readers of Exodus, he thinks of Moses as one "taught all the wisdom [*sophia*] of the Egyptians, powerful in his words and deeds" (Acts 7:22; cf. Heb 11:24–26). A person whose *sophia* led to eloquence and a commitment to justice was the Greco-Roman ideal picture of the political leader, though it had antecedents in the older Near Eastern viewpoint as well. Stephen embellishes the text of Exodus, which does not claim for Moses a high education, to highlight features of Moses, a view he undoubtedly shared with his audience, as comparison with Jewish interpretation of his story shows.[15] He picks up a contrast in

---

15. See the discussion and sources in James Kugel, *The Bible as It Was* (Cambridge: Harvard University Press, 1997), 285–308.

the text by noting, "this very Moses who was addressed by saying, 'who made you an arbitrator and ruler among us?' was the same Moses whom God sent as ruler and rescuer by an angel's hand . . ." (Acts 7:35). Again, a textual clue in Exodus leads to an interpretation in Acts that filters out Moses's reluctance and emphasizes the contrast between Israelite opposition and the divine plan for salvation.

This very contrast, however, causes the sermon to go off the rails, when it turns to Stephen's final peroration. No longer does he speak of *"our* ancestors" but of *"your* ancestors" who were stiff-necked and persecuted the prophets (Acts 7:51–52). He concludes by reporting a vision of Jesus enthroned next to God, a vision that has Jewish precedent but could seem to challenge monotheism itself, hence the core distinction between Judaism (and Christianity) and the pagan world. His hearers, according to Acts, certainly interpret the sermon that way. Shared encyclopedia does not guarantee agreement.

This little example illustrates many things. Modern scholarship often rightly worries about how Stephen's speech and others like it can stoke the flames of antisemitism. That could hardly have been Luke's intention, because Luke-Acts in general and its speeches in particular underscore the continuity between the church's faith in Jesus and its origins in the faith of Israel.[16] The New Testament also emphasizes the continuity between Israel's lack of faith and that potential lack of faith that followers of Jesus can and do have (e.g., 1 Cor 10:1–22). But the potential for such a reading should concern interpreters who must help readers identify with all the parties in the text. The contemporary Christian reader can much more readily assume the role of the slayers of the first martyr than of the man himself.

The content of the encyclopedia of meaning. This possibility of misreading requires that interpreters attend to the content of the shared encyclopedia of meaning. When Eco used that term, he had in mind the type of carefully edited work that emerged in eighteenth-century

16. On the speech's connections to other, often congruent, Jewish interpretations of the biblical stories, see Michael R. Whitenton, "Rewriting Abraham and Joseph: Stephen's Speech (Acts 7:2–16) and Jewish Exegetical Traditions," *NovT* 54 (2012): 149–67; W. Gil Shin, "Integrated Stories and Israel's Contested Worship Space: Exod 15.17 and Stephen's Retelling of Heilsgeschichte (Acts 7)," *NTS* 64 (2018): 495–513; Michal Beth Dinkler, "The Politics of Stephen's Storytelling: Narrative Rhetoric and Reflexivity in Acts 7:2–53," *ZNW* 111 (2020): 33–64.

France as a summary of the major elements of human knowledge. The requirements of print demanded an editorial process of not just distinguishing fact from error but also of assessing the relative importance of facts. The article on Genghis Khan should be longer than that on his son Ögedei, for example. In the current world of the internet encyclopedia, which would require thousands of volumes to print and so could not reasonably be circulated anywhere but on the internet, such a process of assessment becomes much harder to sustain with any degree of consistency. Eco, in short, means by encyclopedia what we used to mean by it. Yet this shift of meaning is itself revealing: the enormous explosion of information over the past thirty years has meant not only the growing possibility of shared knowledge but also, at the same time, the fragmentation of popular knowledge as each of us must, without training or perhaps even desire, become our own editor. The nihilist's creed, "you have your websites and we have ours," has unfortunately come too true.

But what shared knowledge do the biblical stories as transmitted in the church presuppose? The stories of the Bible stake out positions in ancient theological debates and shape ongoing discussions as well. They fashion certain characters in the drama of which humanity is part, and they plot the scenes in that drama.

The characters include first of all the God of Israel who goes under various names: El, El Shaddai, El Elyon, Elohim, Eloah, and especially YHWH. When the Israelite texts written in Hebrew were translated into Greek, this seeming abundance of divine names was rendered as *theos* ("God") and *ho Kyrios* ("the Lord"), already honored titles for deities if not their personal names, among others. Yet the texts of both the Hebrew and Greek Bibles understand these names to denote the selfsame Person, the creator and sustainer of the world who takes a special interest in Israel. The Godhead is neither pluriform, nor at war with itself, nor vulnerable to outside forces. Even texts that ascribe complex human emotions to God—implacable anger or tortured love, for example—do so on such a scale as to raise questions about the adequacy of such language for the deity. The Bible itself sets the stage for the later Jewish and Christian theological ideas of the incomparability, the radical otherness of God. Cultures around the ancient Near East and western Mediterranean shared the view of the godhead as a society analogous to human societies. This view, however, all but disappears in the Hebrew Bible/Old Testament to be replaced by a radical emphasis on the oneness of God.

At the same time, Israel's God is full of mercy toward humanity. Both Old and New Testaments retain the ancient Near Eastern idea that the deity may alternate anger and mercy and must be placated by prayer. As the ancient hymn to Marduk, *Ludlul bēl nēmeqi* ("Let Me Praise the Lord of Wisdom") says, the deity may be "calm in the morning and fierce at night."[17] The God of Israel can be angry at sin but also benevolent toward the suffering and the penitent. Appearances to the contrary, this sense of God's fundamental benevolence pervades the Bible. To take one revealing example, Luke has Jesus enjoining his disciples in the Sermon on the Plain to "be merciful as your Father is merciful" (Luke 6:36). The label "merciful" (Greek: *oiktirmōn*) is the normal LXX translation of the Hebrew epithet *rahum*, a label that applies to God as part of a larger phrase "gracious and merciful."[18] That is, Jesus merely summarizes a viewpoint already centuries old and fundamental to the religion of Israel and its descendants, Judaism and Christianity.

The God of Israel has enjoyed a long relationship with a people, a history that goes through phases that various biblical writers describe in terms of promises made and kept, or legally as a covenant, or as a monarchy with a divine ruler and protector alongside human subjects enjoying a sort of family relationship to that ruler. Israel's association with God could be understood in different ways, but they all come together as one of mutual relationship, marked by the exchange of gifts. God grants land, food, family, and all the preconditions of happiness, and humans offer all they can offer, prayer and generous treatment of each other. That vision of humanity takes many turns but it consistently involves real human beings with all our capacity for good and evil.

The relationship is chiefly expressed on the human side in terms of obedience to Torah, applying to the people of Israel and not to Gentiles. However, contrary to the popular Protestant view of law as an alien force that confronts us in our sin and reminds us of our failure, in the Old Testament law is a gift, a way of life in which humans may find delight

---

17. W. G. Lambert, *Babylonian Wisdom Literature* (Oxford: Clarendon, 1960), 21–62.

18. See Exod 34:5–6; 2 Chron 30:9; Neh 9:17, 31; Pss 86:15–16; 111:4; 112:4; 145:8; Joel 2:12–14; Jon 4:2; cf. Jas 5:11. This attribute for God is one of the most common in Israel's texts and therefore the church's Bible.

because loyalty is extended to the God who freed the people from Egyptian slavery. God's rule is not a tyranny but the good governance of an extended family. While some biblical texts question the goodness of God's rule (Job; Lamentations), the preponderant view of biblical texts emphasizes divine benevolence and providential care.

The Plot and Its Characters, Again

Identifying the plotline of the Christian Bible is not the same as performing it, and performance does not require that the audience accept every part of the story without question.[19] In fact, the performance demands that the audience interrogate the story, asking questions about its trustworthiness as an account of reality. We inevitably ask questions about the moral integrity of the characters (including God), hence about their motives and the results of their actions. Contrary to the view that storytelling is a fundamentally orienting activity that builds group solidarity at the expense of independent thought, the realities of the biblical story seem to point in the other direction. Because it consistently insists on the audience's participation in the performance, the need to interrogate the story is built in.

But interrogate how? The biblical text includes examples of what it thinks of as both proper and improper ways of questioning the story. Amos speaks of those who improperly defy the moral implications of the exodus story through their abuse of power and their greed, which extends even to the silencing of critical voices (Amos 2:9–16). The Sermon on the Mount similarly reminds Jesus's listeners that when they embrace peacemaking, hunger for righteousness, and all the rest, they will meet opposition, "for in the same way they persecuted the prophets" (Matt 5:11–12; cf. Luke 6:23). The Psalter summarizes the human potential for embracing injustice as a denial of God and criticizes such a self-absorbed disregard for basic morality as the attitude of those who say, "There is no God" (Pss 14:1; 53:1). The counter-story that the Psalter rejects does not involve theoretical atheism, a much more

---

19. The relationship of the plotline of the Christian Bible to that of the Jewish Bible lies beyond the scope of our discussion. Though different, these two narratives do closely interrelate, and Christians may enrich our understanding of the work of God by considering that alternative understanding with care and respect.

modern phenomenon, but any approach to life that denies a morality above human appetite.

So, some forms of questioning the story are out of bounds from the point of view of the biblical texts, but others remain very much in bounds. Nehemiah 9 recounts a long penitential prayer that repeatedly admits to the failings of the ancestors, recounting Israel's history in detail as one disaster after another, but still concludes at the end that "we are still slaves in our own land" (Neh 9:36), a fact that the ones praying believe unjust. Or in a different vein, the book of Revelation presents John in his wanderings through the theater of heaven needing reassurance about the fate of the martyrs for the faith. The character articulates the readers' doubts and the hoped-for reassurances of God. More pointedly, books like Lamentations and Job bluntly articulate their creators' questions about divine providence without offering resolution, either in this life or (as in Revelation) the next.

Walter Brueggemann famously attempted to frame the Old Testament's approach to story as testimony, counter-testimony, and found testimony. His reasoning is essentially reactive, as he tried to avoid both historicism, with its obsessions with verifying "what really happened," and ontology, the focus on "being."[20] Despite its many suggestive elements in detail, such an approach raises many questions, not least how one distinguishes among various kinds of speech about God (center and periphery), the appropriateness of testimony as a metaphor for such speech, the referentiality of such speech (is Brueggemann's God a fictional character?), and even the nature of the pluralism his project evokes.[21]

Nevertheless, his attempt to focus a theological reading of the Old Testament on Israel's story of God's interaction with itself and the world is surely on the right track, as is his insistence that the story requires reexamination rather than rote recitation. On the other hand, his eschewal of ontology seems a serious error, not only because it breaks with the long Jewish and Christian concern about how and to what extent the biblical text is true, but because it opens the door,

---

20. Walter Brueggemann, *Theology of the Old Testament: Testimony, Dispute, Advocacy* (Minneapolis: Fortress, 1997), 714.

21. On the last point, see Jon Levenson, "Is Brueggemann Really a Pluralist?" *Harvard Theological Review* 93 (2000): 265–94.

unintentionally in all likelihood, to the very sorts of anti-pluralism that Brueggemann wishes to avoid. To put it bluntly, mainline Protestants do not have to worry about the same abuses of the story those of us in more conservative churches do. Christian nationalism has found a home in evangelical churches to an alarming degree, for example. It is possible to read biblical texts imaginatively in ways that careen off the rails into a kind of culture-hatred that celebrates some of the ugliest sides of human nature. Imagination alone cannot guarantee good results unless readers of the Bible attend to the story's truthfulness, part of which must be a response to realities to which it refers, not simply its internal logic.

Pursuing this point would take us too far afield, however. For now, it suffices to say that our approach to the church as storyteller assumes that something happened in the real world in Jesus Christ as the sign that God keeps the promises to Israel and through Israel to the world, and that Israel's story, into which Gentiles have also been grafted, continues to bear fruit for the communities that perform it diligently and creatively.

How do we do that?

The Power of Storytelling in Christian Formation

If we accept that storytelling goes so far back in human history that it has become a shared linguistic practice in all cultures, that the story-telling event includes not just the words of the story (with characters, plot developments, scenery, etc.) but also the performance itself, the storyteller, and the audience, and that all stories refer to prior stories and a shared knowledge of the world, then we can begin to think about how the church can tell the Bible's story as part of its own story with renewed vigor.

Of course, there are many ways to tell a story. In a given day, any of us can watch a movie, read a novel or history book, listen to a podcast, look intently at a painting, or chat with friends over coffee, among other storytelling events. Story is everywhere. Yet, like other things that are everywhere, problematizing the storytelling event is important. In doing so, we can both distinguish unskilled from skilled practices, and also identify the ethical dimensions of storytelling. Master storytellers can induct their hearers into an awareness of evil as well as good, after all.

Harry Potter needs his Voldemort, Esther and Mordecai their Haman, and, as the Apostles' and Constantinopolitan Creeds insist, Jesus his Pontius Pilate.

In their brief comments on teaching psychology through storytelling, Landrum, Brakke, and McCarthy argue that storytelling has four purposes: to "(a) create student interest; (b) provide a structure for remembering course material; (c) share information in a familiar and accessible form; and (d) create a more personal student-teacher connection."[22] In short, teaching through story allows for cognitive gains in the student as well as improving solidarity between teacher and student, thereby creating the atmosphere of trust necessary for learning to occur. Storytelling enriches a learning environment, whatever the "subject" under consideration.

In the church's life, the performance of the biblical story has always involved the intersection of the written text with orality, as multiple media of storytelling have played themselves out. By telling and hearing stories, the church community can empower and humanize others and foster empathy and understanding. Stories can repair or heal broken human dignity and can inspire human beings to create a brighter community. Good stories explore motivation and decision-making. For example, why did Joseph's brothers sell him? Why did he forgive them? Why did Tamar try to honor her deceased husband by bearing children, even when the family into which she had married had little use for her? The church exploring the last parts of Genesis, to take one biblical text, might well ask such questions and attempt to answer them even when the biblical text does not do so directly.

In her stimulating study of storytelling as a mode of religious education, Susan Shaw proposes that we understand storytelling in the church in two ways. First, it is "a context in which to understand the parameters of intellectual and theoretical exploration and the relationship of theological understandings to lived faith."[23] To gloss her point, we should say that the second-order thinking of theological reflection

22. R. Eric Landrum, Karen Brakke, and Maureen A. McCarthy, "The Pedagogical Power of Storytelling," *Scholarship of Teaching and Learning in Psychology* 5/3 (2019): 248 (247–53).

23. Susan M. Shaw, *Storytelling in Religious Education* (Birmingham, AL: Religious Education Press, 1999), 82.

does not occur in an abstract story-free world, but one where God, Jesus, the prophets, and the saints are living characters with their own stories that intertwine with those of the church telling them. Theological reflection exists in a dynamic, mutually reinforcing relationship with the biblical story.

Second, Shaw says, "Stories provide the grammatical setting for religious convictions."[24] If we change her word "grammatical" to "syntactical," we would probably be closer to her intended point. The stories of the Bible and the church provide the basic syntax through which the church speaks. The characters and plotlines of the biblical story do not stand in for abstract ideas. Sharing and living our faith stories connects us to the faithfulness of God.

In short, through the combination of social and linguistic metaphors to create a sociolinguistic understanding of storytelling, Shaw signals an important dimension of the church's practices with the Bible (even though her concern for storytelling is wider than "just" the Bible). The biblical stories provide a language through which the church can begin to understand itself and its relationships to others, including God.

We obviously must be careful here. It is undoubtedly true that stories can heal as long as they promote empathy and understanding. The biblical stories can often function that way. Yet the necessity of their doing so is not guaranteed by the stories themselves. Friends of ours from Croatia reported to us during our last visit there how a former president of the country had used the stories about the elimination of the Canaanites in Joshua and Judges to justify reprisals against the Serbs during the wars of the 1990s, for example. That is, as Miroslav Volf has pointed out using very closely related examples, memory (hence storytelling about historical events) can be distorted toward bad ends.[25] It seems that for storytelling to be constructive, a whole ecology of thought and action is required. Story forms moral commitments but does not do so alone.

24. Shaw, *Storytelling*, 83.
25. Miroslav Volf, *The End of Memory: Remembering Rightly in a Violent World*, 2nd ed. (Grand Rapids: Eerdmans, 2021).

The Locations of Storytelling

How is such an ecology formed? Moral commitments are formed through human interaction and reflection in contexts. It is no wonder, then, that the biblical story has been told in many settings. The Christian congregation is one, and the family another. It is difficult to return to the confidence of the nineteenth-century pastor and theologian Horace Bushnell, who wished that children would grow up thinking of themselves as Christians without any sense of a break from their surroundings.[26] The intact Christendom of nineteenth-century New England simply does not exist anymore. Still, we probably need not go as far as Tom Beaudoin in his provocative consideration of "a kind of Christian parenting that does not further Christian affiliation."[27] When our friend Kathy told her children Bible stories in the car as they drove home from school, she was not compelling them to be Christians. She was affording them the opportunity to make an informed choice later in life.

The family dinner table can be a place for the Bible without trying to return to the old Scotch Presbyterian Sabbath, with its silence and immobility, against which generations of now "liberated" Protestants have reacted so strongly. The family devotional can surely be a vibrant place for families to reconnect with each other around their core values and beliefs, away from the tyranny of social media or the addiction of the streaming service of choice.

Another location can be a revitalized Sunday school. Most Protestant churches of whatever theological commitments have experienced the sharp decline of the Sunday school as it evolved away from lectures and lessons toward a social hour. The sacrament of doughnuts and coffee has become the one indispensable ingredient of this vestige of earlier practices. Yet the Sunday school began in the 1780s as an opportunity to educate poor children in basic literacy as well as the Bible. Deep in the Sunday school's DNA lies a commitment to equity of opportunity, to basic norms of human decency, and to learning. Now in a world of innumerable podcasts and e-books, when all the knowledge (and,

26. Horace Bushnell, *Views of Christian Nurture, and of Subjects Adjacent Thereto* (Hartford, CT: Hunt, 1847).

27. Tom Beaudoin, "Why Does Practice Matter Theologically?" in *Conundrums in Practical Theology*, ed. Joyce Ann Mercer and Bonnie J. Miller-McLemore (Leiden: Brill, 2016), 8 (8–32).

alas, misinformation) of the world lies a few clicks away, we persist in practices that lack social depth or intellectual creativity, even when the opportunity to do better lies close by.

Yet even in an institution as decrepit as many Sunday schools, revitalization is possible if we recount the story of the Bible in ways that invite children and adults to learn together. As Walter Brueggemann pointed out in one of his early books, storytelling and other means of passing on faith from adults to children are acts of gift giving. Children "receive" a story of redemption from the compassionate care of their parents and other adults. Children "connect" the ancient stories to their own lives and so acquire ways of "celebrating" those stories through ritual at holidays that foreground acts of charity. And children themselves become storytellers as they learn to contribute acts of mercy to the community's life.[28] Storytelling, in short, inducts the young into the life of those older.

To rise to such a desired outcome, most churches need to carve out more times for storytelling. The National Council of Churches advocates for spiritual practices that aid the practice of justice, including *lectio divina*, the slow reading of biblical texts. The United States Conference of Catholic Bishops promotes Bible study in the home and in group studies, providing significant resources for that work. Likewise, evangelicals often write about the need to translate the biblical story into the parables and proverbs of a local culture. So Kelly Malone speaks of the need to rethink the Gospels' stories to avoid portraying Jesus as a sorcerer to Japanese audiences.[29] Peter Ochs and his colleagues have developed a textual practice in which Jews, Christians, and Muslims read each other's sacred texts and discuss them respectfully yet searchingly.[30] And there are many other practices worth noting and celebrating. Some of these take on the color of a particular denominational or social setting, but many readily translate across the boundaries that

28. Walter Brueggemann, *Belonging and Growing in the Christian Community* (Crawfordsville, IN: PCUSA, 1979), 31–32.

29. Kelly Malone, "The Power of Biblical Storytelling," *Evangelical Missions Quarterly* 50 (2014): 314–20.

30. Most recently, Peter Ochs and David F. Ford, *Religion without Violence: The Practice and Philosophy of Scriptural Reasoning* (Eugene, OR: Cascade, 2019); Peter Ochs, *The Return to Scripture: Essays in Postcritical Scriptural Interpretation* (Eugene, OR: Wipf & Stock, 2008).

Christianity drew between the sixteenth and nineteenth centuries, and is now scrubbing away. In short, the resources for reinvigorating the telling of, and engagement with, the biblical story lie at hand if we will put them to work. Storytelling can occur in many settings whenever groups of Christians come together.

The Media of Storytelling

In the church's two-thousand-year life, the biblical story has been told through many means. Christians copied, read aloud, discussed, and memorized the Bible in small groups and large assemblies beginning already in the first century. Painters, and later sculptors, vivified the stories. Composers set them to music. But beyond generalities, it makes sense to give some indication of how storytelling might work in the church.

As a boy, Mark grew up in a small church in which children learned the basic stories of the Bible. The women who taught children—and the teachers were mostly women—had them memorize the stops in Paul's missionary journeys in the book of Acts, the names of the apostles, the basic storyline of Genesis and other parts of the Bible. They would often have them draw maps or pictures illustrating those bits of memorized data. Although that sort of learning has often come under assault in more recent approaches to religious education, there is much to commend it. Children can learn stories well, and forming a mind well stocked with such details hardly seems like a criminal activity. Perhaps we have misunderstood the ranking of learning practices in Bloom's Taxonomy, forgetting that memorization, because it's at the bottom of the pile, is foundational rather than substandard. Many professions rely heavily on memorization as a first step in learning. Think of courses in human anatomy and physiology that every prospective nurse or doctor must take, or how airplane pilots must learn what all the dials mean, or how actors learn scripts. Memorization is not sufficient, but it is necessary.

Other media also help. David Price describes the first mass-produced biblical art from the early sixteenth century workshops of Dürer, Cranach, and Merian, as attempts "to make biblical art the core of Renaissance humanist culture, a source for political and religious reflection as well as aesthetic experience, appealing . . . to the 'God-fearing' and the 'art-loving' in equal measure."[31] Dürer's woodcuts of the Apocalypse, for example, brought to life the book's drama of divine defeat of chaos and evil. His pictures and their many descendants probably have influenced the church's interpretation of the work more than any number of commentaries and scholarly monographs, or all of them combined. Similarly, Cranach's systematic illustration of much of the Bible opened the door to a flood of imitators and competitors that has not really abated. The spread of biblical literacy went hand in hand with the spread of a visual literacy that reinforced, rather than displaced, the oral storytelling that had also accompanied written texts during the period prior to the invention of the printing press and the creation of mass media. In the past 125 years, movies have carried much of the responsibility of stimulating our visual imaginations about these stories.[32] Sometimes, the picture can misshape the imagination, as when Cecil B. Demille's 1956 *Ten Commandments* conflated democratic patriotism with the biblical story, but at least the images on the screen (as on the page) can stimulate thinking.

A more recent but highly effective medium of storytelling is the case study. Teaching through cases began in the nineteenth century at law and medical schools and reached theology only in the 1970s and 1980s, where it has still not taken hold. Yet the use of cases (see the appendix) allows students of the Bible to explore the contingency behind the stories. We can ask about the motivations of Paul and his opponents at Corinth, their points of agreement and disagreement, and the options available to them rather than simply blindly accepting either one or the other side of the argument. Or to take the case that appears in the appendix, we might consider the conflict reported in Jeremiah 44 involving the refugees from Judah in Egypt, who must decide just what part of their history deserves bringing forward, that is, how to think about their story in ways that could underwrite future actions (or foreclose them).

---

31. David H. Price, *In the Beginning Was the Image: Art and the Reformation Bible* (Oxford: Oxford University Press, 2021), 331.

32. For a good introduction, see, for example, Adele Reinhartz, *The Bible and Cinema: An Introduction* (London: Routledge, 2013).

In engaging a story, it is important to identify the characters, their actions, their quests, the obstacles they must overcome, and so on.[33] But other relevant concerns address the moral values of the characters and the narrator, the vision(s) of God implicit or explicit in the text, the places where the text's view of reality clashes with our own, and the interplay between its values and ours. The case study invites readers into the world of the Bible through a process of open dialogue.

In other words, to return to Shaw's point, storytelling both forms an environment for thought about deep issues and provides language for expressing that thought. Story does not necessarily force the audience into a singular decision: we may find unacceptable Hebrews 11's naming of Jephthah as a hero of faith or wonder if killing the Egyptian firstborn as an act of poetic justice was the only available option in a moment of liberation of the Israelite slaves (perhaps it was). But that is the point. Story invites wonder, argument, conversation, and, at last, choice. And case studies are one way to highlight that aspect of their functioning in a human community like the church.

On Storytelling

The discussion of the medium of storytelling should be taken as an invitation to tell the biblical story creatively, not to substitute another story for it. The message cannot, contrary to the cliché, be reduced to the medium. Yet the variety of media through which the church has told the story of the Bible over the centuries, and the myriad ways therefore in which Christians have understood the story, raise the question of precisely what story we are telling ourselves.

At the deepest level, the act of storytelling is itself the story. The church is a community that tells a story about itself as an heir of Israel. The story involves divine mercy beginning with creation in a garden and ending with new creation in a city where the tree of life has reappeared, this time "for the healing of the nations." The *Catechism of the Catholic Church* puts things nicely when it says, "the Christian faith is not a 'religion of the book.' Christianity is the religion of the 'Word' of God, a word which is 'not a written and mute word, but the Word which

33. A good introductory list of questions appears in J. P. Fokkelman, *Reading Biblical Narrative: An Introductory Guide* (Louisville: Westminster John Knox, 1999).

is incarnate and living.'"[34] This view is not very far from Karl Barth's statement in the *Church Dogmatics* that "preaching and the sacrament of the Church do indeed need the basis and authority and authenticity of the original Word of God in Scripture to be the Word of God. But Scripture also needs proclamation by preaching and sacrament, for it wills to be read and understood and expounded and the Word of God attested in it wills to have actuality."[35] That is, a broad consensus exists in Christian theology that the Bible's status as God's Word derives from Christ's authority as its interpreter and the recipient of its promises, and the Bible comes to life in the church's proclamation and sacramental practices. Storytelling thus fits into a larger theological framework as a means of not just encoding the good news in linguistic form but of recalling to the church its life with its Lord and helping the church live that life. The characters in the biblical story live alongside us because, like them, we play roles in the same drama of redemption.

We may well imagine with Elie Wiesel that God created humanity out of a love of story, but of course we do not know all the Deity's reasons for doing so. Perhaps the British novelist and documentary writer Tahir Shah gets closer to the truth when he makes one of his characters say, "The stories make us what we are. . . . The storytellers keep the flame of our culture alive. . . . They teach us about our ancestors, and give our children the values they will need—a sense of honor and chivalry, and they teach what is right and what is wrong."[36] If we take the money metaphor seriously, then we see stories as a store of value, a medium of exchange, and a tool of valuation. They do all those things, and the Bible's story is no exception. How does the church bring that story to life? That is the subject of the next chapter.

34. *Catechism of the Catholic Church*, 2nd ed. (Vatican City: Libreria Editrice Vaticana, 2019), ¶108. The latter quotation is from St. Bernard of Clairvaux.

35. Karl Barth, *Church Dogmatics* 1.2, trans. Geoffrey W. Bromiley, 2nd ed. (Edinburgh: T&T Clark, 1975), 501.

36. Tahir Shah, *In Arabian Nights: A Caravan of Moroccan Dreams* (New York: Bantam, 2008), 18.

CHAPTER 4

Biblical Ritual in Context

In her 2020 film *Nomadland*, Frances McDormand plays Fern, a widow who left the company town of Empire, Nevada after jobs in the local gypsum mine dried up and her husband died. Without family to live with or a house to live in, Fern takes to the road, joining other nomads. She proclaims herself not "homeless" but "houseless," as her van becomes both her shelter from the elements and her mode of transportation. She finds relationships in temporary jobs and, more significantly, in the gatherings of fellow nomads who never say a final goodbye to one another but wait until the next rendezvous.

Among her friends is an older woman named Swankie, who is dying of inoperable cancer but prefers to see the beauties of the world rather than receive treatments that will only prolong life, not enrich it. After Swankie dies, Fern and Swankie's other friends gather one last time. As Swankie had said in one of their last meetings, "Maybe when I die, my friends will gather around the fire and toss a rock into the fire in memory of me." They do. Seated in a circle around the sparking campfire, each arises in turn to pitch a rock into the blaze. "Because she loved rocks," says one friend. "See you down the road, Swankie," says another. At last the camera follows the sparks ascending into the night sky and then cuts to the next morning's daybreak over the austere desert landscape. "See you down the road" becomes a word of hope for possible future gatherings. Perhaps this life is not the end.

The poignant scene captures a moment of ritual, the second modality of life we wish to discuss. If humans are by nature tellers of stories, wrestling with characters and lives other than our own as a window into ourselves, we also are inveterate creators of ritual. We long to express the inexpressible, to celebrate or mourn, to commemorate and reenact the past, to invoke the future. We love to explore the possibilities of symbol-making by moving ourselves and various objects around. Rituals take many forms and trigger many associations. They metamorphose as communities do, responding not only to deep primal needs and desires but also the proximate and personal. We all do them, almost every day.

In the previous chapter, we discussed the ritual in Deuteronomy 26:1–10. In expressing gratitude for the bounty of the land, Israelite farmers were to tell a story that connected their own version of the proximate and the personal, not to the primordial, but to the story of Israel as a particular group. They recount the story in the company of a designated person (the priest), at a designated time, for a designated reason, and as part of a series of movements in the company of others. The story of the exodus and the events preceding and following it repeated itself each time a family had enjoyed enough to eat and celebrated its good fortune together.

This interest in ritual is not unique to Deuteronomy within the Bible, of course. Rather, it permeates Jewish and Christian Scripture precisely because the communities who use those texts do so in the context of ritual. They read Scripture in connection with the daily and weekly life of prayer and song in assemblies on Sabbath or Sunday. They also bring it forward during major holidays like Passover or Easter. Not only do the biblical texts contain many forms of ritual texts, but the entirety comes to life when read, recited, or sung by communities in connections with gestures, movements, and the choreography of human bodies in space dedicated to worship. Every Sunday, the church performs the descendants of these rituals as they have developed through the interaction of scriptural texts and unfolding contexts. This reality of the Bible's life deserves more attention than it sometimes receives, especially from Christians whose theology, influenced by the Enlightenment's narrowing of the scope of reason, downplays or even denies the role of the body in the life of the spirit. All of that requires further attention.

Here we wish to argue that the ubiquity of ritual in the Bible and the use of the Bible in ritual speak to an ongoing need in the church's life. That need can be neglected or ignored but only to the detriment of the church and its members. Education for and through ritual equips the community to be itself, to live out its key values and commitments, to have a healthy relationship with its own past, and to anticipate its future with hope and joy. Ritual's transformative power stems from the unity of intellect and feeling in the performances of symbol by a community.

This all happens because rituals deal in the world of symbols, signs that point in some way to other things. Ritual practices invite persons at many levels of understanding and commitment to work together toward a common goal. The sharp social boundaries separating children, the elderly, or those with different neurological or motor skills from others more or less dissolve in the world of ritual. And rituals that are most central to a community's life invite ever deeper reflection and so provide a source of wisdom.

To substantiate these sweeping claims, we construct this chapter in several steps: laying out the nature of ritual from a history-of-religions and Christian theological perspective; describing the evolution of certain rituals (especially those associated with Passover and Eucharist, and sacrifice more generally); analyzing the role of prayer as a dimension of the church's (and Israel's) ritual life; and thinking through how the retrieval of a more robust ritual mindset might benefit the church's life.

The Nature of Ritual

To begin, we should pause to clarify a term. Having used the word "ritual" several times already, we should try to clarify what we mean by it. There are many possibilities, reflecting the prior commitments of scholars studying them. For example, Paul Pettitt, who specializes in the archaeology of the Stone Age, speaks of ritual as "defined from an archaeological perspective at least as habitual manifestations of religious beliefs which may leave material remains in the archaeological record."[1] That materialist definition fits the study of past human beings who produced no texts and whose beliefs are mostly lost to us, but it also reveals an important feature of ritual for all periods: it alters the physical world in large or small ways. Humans inhabit space, and ritual organizes that space in ways that allow a community's beliefs and values to have vitality.

Consider a more influential and helpful example. In an extended reflection on ritual, Catherine Bell proposes to define the term by means of what she calls a "practice approach." This view, which we find very

---

1. Paul Pettitt, "Religion and Ritual in the Lower and Middle Palaeolithic," in *Oxford Handbook of the Archaeology of Ritual and Religion*, ed. Timothy Insoll (Oxford: Oxford University Press, 2011), 330.

congenial, invites us to do three things at least: to analyze ritual "in its real context, which is the full spectrum of ways of acting within any given context"; to recognize "the primacy of the body moving about within a specially constructed space"; and to understand "ritualization" as "a way of acting that tends to promote the authority of forces deemed to derive from beyond the immediate situation."[2] That is, ritual is an action that involves human bodies moving about within a prescribed space to evoke divine, human, or other realities beyond the humans and their actions immediately involved. Ritual cannot occur only in our heads. It employs all the senses as it draws in the whole person.

Of course, not all rituals are religious, if by "religion" we mean something to do with supernatural beings. But they all connect us to something bigger than ourselves.

Roy Rappaport is even more succinct in defining ritual as "the performance of a more or less invariant sequence of formal acts and utterances not entirely encoded by the performers."[3] This definition, which is close to Bell's, understands ritual to concern bodily movement structured independently of the emotions or whims of those doing them at the moment. We cannot just think about ritual, we must do it. It cannot be a free-for-all but must tap into a community's memories, values, and self-understandings in some way.

Christian theology can profit from ritual studies in many ways, but it also needs to focus the discussion in explicitly Christian ways. We think of the following as an adequate starting point: "Christian ritual is a set of actions, words, and movements performed by the church to reflect its considered understanding of the experience of communion with the God of Moses and Jesus Christ." In making this turn, we resist significant trends in religious studies to downplay the ideas operating within rituals in favor of an emphasis on practice. But going against the grain seems reasonable in this case precisely because the focus is upon a Christian engagement with the Bible's views of ritual. We seek to fashion a dialogue between the contemporary churches and their Scriptures. So we might well ask, how does the Bible explicate ritual,

2. Catherine Bell, *Ritual: Perspectives and Dimensions* (New York: Oxford University Press, 1997), 81–82.
3. Roy Rappaport, *Ritual and Religion in the Making of Humanity* (Cambridge: Cambridge University Press, 1999), 24.

how does Scripture function in Christian rituals, and what should we learn from the answers to these two questions?

Passover and Eucharist

The answer to that first question must involve a description of the various approaches to ritual visible in the Christian Bible. Even a cursory reading of the text reveals the surprising frequency of mentions of human beings performing ritual in all sorts of circumstances. These range from thanksgiving for safe births (Ruth 4:13–17; 1 Sam 1:21–27) to weddings (Gen 29:21–30; Ruth 4:11–12) and funerals (2 Sam 3:31–35; 2 Chron 35:24–25). Rituals may be private and individualized, as when Ruth swears to enter Naomi's ritual world of worship and burial (Ruth 1:16–17) but ends up adding to it the communal experience of childbirth (Ruth 4:13–17). Or it may include the entire community en masse, as in several events of covenant renewal in the Deuteronomistic History (Josh 24:1–28; 1 Sam 7:1–6) and other communal assemblies (Neh 8:1–9:37).

More frequently, ritual works at levels in between these two notional extremes. Early on, the Israelite tradition identified three annual holidays that coincided with transitions in the agricultural year (Unleavened Bread/Passover, Pentecost or Shavuot, and Tabernacles or Sukkot). This short list of three holidays gradually expanded to structure most of the year (Exod 23:14–19; Lev 23; Num 28–29; Esther 9:20–32; 1 Macc 4:36–59), adding the holidays of Rosh Hashanah, Yom Kippur, Hanukkah, and Purim. The weekly celebration of the Sabbath became a defining marker of the community, certainly during the early Second Temple period if not earlier. Ritual came to shape time, social relationships, and communal memories for the Israelite community.

Moreover, each holiday acts as a sort of ritual magnet, attracting more and more layers of meaning as it roots a community in its own story. Traditions that flourish today are like archaeological tells. They embed layers of meaning that originated sometimes centuries apart but have fused together over time.

Passover. A good example of such growth is the festival of Passover. Many scholars believe that it began as a merger of an old spring agricultural festival (Unleavened Bread) and a specifically Israelite celebration of the exodus. That may be right, but most biblical texts begin with the association already in place. That is, the holiday finds a warrant not just in the cycles of nature, theologically significant as those can be, but in an event lodged firmly in Israel's collective memory. Yet even there, the ritual instructions undergo modification over time, as a comparison between Exodus and Deuteronomy, two of the earliest extended discussions, shows:

And YHWH said to Moses and to Aaron in the land of Egypt, "This month will be for you the first month, and will be the first of the year's months. Say to all the assembly of Israel, 'On the tenth of this month, they should each take for themselves a sheep for a patrimonial house, a sheep for a household. And if the household is too small for a sheep, they and the nearest neighbor to their house, taking account of the number of household members, counting the number of mouths for eating a sheep. It should be a flawless sheep, male, a year old for you. You may take it from either the sheep or the goats.'"
(Exod 12:1–5)

Observe the month of Aviv and make the Passover to YHWH your God, for in the month of Aviv, YHWH your God brought you from Egypt at night. And you should sacrifice the Passover [sacrifice] to YHWH your God, whether from the flock or the herd, in the place where YHWH will choose to set his name. You should not eat leaven during it for seven days. During it, you should eat unleavened bread, the bread of affliction—for you came hurriedly from the land of Egypt—so you may remember the day you came from the land of Egypt, all the days of your life. No trace should be seen in all your territory during the seven days. None of the flesh that you sacrifice should remain during the evening of the first day until the morning (of the next). You should not sacrifice the Passover in one of your gates [i.e., settlements] that YHWH your God is giving you.
(Deut 16:1–5)

The two instructions overlap a great deal and clearly describe the same recurring festival. They do not differ markedly in rationale. But Deuteronomy, in keeping with its overall theological agenda, moves the sacrifice of the Passover lamb or kid to a single location, the central sanctuary at which all sacrifice is to take place. That is, as a text with explicitly educational aims, Deuteronomy seeks to reform Israel's village- and family-based religion by removing the practice of sacrifice from the Levites in the villages to the one central temple. That move was part of a larger one that entrusted instruction in the ways of God to those local priests. However, as a result of Deuteronomy's intended reform, any local celebration of the Passover became something other than a sacrifice, and the potential for a serious problem arose. More on that in a moment.

Prior to taking up that point, it is important to notice the ritual aspects of the Passover meal. These texts long predate the rich ritual development of the Passover seder, with the recitation of story, the delightfully meaningful game of the *afikomen*, and the educational question, "why is this day different?" These texts live nearer the taproot of the holiday, focusing on the ritual of the meal itself but also adding some interpretations that later bear even greater fruit.

Exodus lays out the basic bit: the ritual occurs in the context of the family and involves a meal centered on a sheep or a goat, animals associated with the pastoralist life of Canaan rather than the cattle-breeding of Egypt. Since males are more expendable for good husbandry, the animal eaten is male and young. The selection and killing of the animal occur at the same time for all the community, however, indicating that families exist in a larger communal network (which is why a small family may make a pragmatic decision to share food with another small family). Just the basics of the meal appear, setting forth the movement of bodies (human and animal) within prescribed spaces and pointing toward meanings (exodus, deliverance of the community) and beings (God) not confined to the space or feelings of the families involved (as Rappaport would remind us).[4]

However, Deuteronomy makes an important change, and that change creates a problem. Since Deuteronomy has decreed that sacrifice may occur only in the central sanctuary, it now must insist that if the Passover meal is a sacrifice, it must be eaten at the temple. This creates all sorts of practical problems that Deuteronomy itself does not solve. Must a family living too far away eat a vegan Passover? What if the sanctuary lay in ruins or disappeared altogether? The text does not address such problems directly.

But Deuteronomy also adds layers of meaning, reflecting on the exodus story itself. It calls the unleavened bread, a perfectly palatable and nutritious food in its own right, the "bread of affliction" to

4. Rappaport, *Ritual and Religion*, 24.

emphasize the haste of the first Passover celebrants' flight. This is a bit puzzling, however. Why not call it "the bread of haste"? Why "affliction"? The answer must be that the haste itself betokens the overall situation, the danger that the Israelites will face in the exodus story until they leave the land ahead of a homicidal, and by this point deranged, Pharaoh. That is, the name of the ritual element evokes a key dimension of the original story, even when Deuteronomy does not explicate the connection in detail. The bread signifies oppression, and eating it allows the community, whether it is now oppressed or not, to empathize with the suffering of others and celebrate the reality, or at least the possibility, of deliverance. The compression of meaning, of which ritual is capable, occurs here.

Other biblical texts about Passover/Unleavened Bread speak of it as a pilgrimage festival or *hag* (Lev 23:3–8; 2 Chron 30; Ezek 45:21–24; Ezra 6:13–22), and that seems to have been the original reality (see Exod 23:15 on the Feast of Unleavened Bread). Pilgrimage would be relatively easy in a nation with many local religious sites, as Israel and Judah were before Josiah's reforms in the south during the late sixth century BCE. Traveling to the family homestead would be less burdensome than other options and, in fact, an opportunity for reunions and remembrances, much like a modern holiday gathering for many families. Deuteronomy's theology changes the practical nature of the festival, however. If it is to be a pilgrimage feast, it must always occur at one destination, Jerusalem, the location Deuteronomy seems to identify as "the place where YHWH will put his name."

Ironically, Deuteronomy's insistence on sacrifice only at the one central sanctuary opened the door to the later development of Passover/Unleavened Bread as a family event available wherever a Jewish community exists. The meal ceases to be a sacrifice, but evokes the ancient practice nevertheless. Deuteronomy opened that door by pushing hard on the need to instruct Israelite children and adults in how to worship the one God and how to interact with other human beings.

The Eucharist. A different but related ritual in the Christian Bible is the Eucharist. Though different Christian groups observe it differently and with varying understandings, they all shape a space around a table that contains bread and wine (or unfermented grape juice in some traditions), which the worshipers share in ways very different from ordinary meals (even the most festive) in order both to recall the Last Supper and the whole passion of Jesus and to foreshadow the final resolution of all things in the eschaton. Bits of food and more or less familiar words shape an experience that worshipers understand to connect them to God.

For Christians, the Lord's Supper, or Eucharist, derives from the earlier festival of Passover/Unleavened Bread. Some of the most ancient Christian texts trace the weekly practice back to Jesus's celebration of the Passover (Matt 26:17–30 = Mark 14:12–25 = Luke 22:7–23). While the Gospel of John does not depict the institution of the Eucharist as a scene in Jesus's last week, it adopts the language of Passover for Jesus himself as he becomes the paschal lamb (John 19:34). John's use of Passover as a sort of allegory for the passion of Jesus extends to his quotation of Exod 12:46 ("not a bone of it shall be broken") in John 19:36, with Jesus becoming the Passover sacrifice. That move may also have an intervening element, since the same line occurs in Ps 34:20 as a description of how God protects an innocent sufferer. In John, Jesus becomes that sufferer as well as the sacrifice. (It does not follow that the psalm writer intentionally quoted Exodus, merely that the coincidence of language suggested a connection to the Fourth Evangelist as an interpreter of the whole Bible.)

What is more, the figural reading of Jesus as a stand-in for the Passover lamb appears also in Paul, who calls Jesus "our *pascha*" and exhorts the Corinthians to expunge the "leaven" of sin from their lives (1 Cor 5:7–8). Since the divine Passover has already occurred, at the first Easter, the followers of Jesus should live in a perpetual state of remembrance of God's saving act. In Paul's thinking, the Eucharist is on the way to the later understanding of it as a sacrifice, a view that dominated Christian theology for centuries until the Protestant Reformation questioned it. For Paul (and John), the Lord's Supper evokes Jesus's sacrifice for all. The meal brings to life a community sharing a common history of sin and redemption and a common eschatological hope. The shared life around the communal meal thins out and eventually dissolves the sharp social distinctions that societies create outside the context of Christian congregation.

As some of the heirs of this rich environment of ritual practice and reflection on practice, the primitive church could draw on a range of metaphors for understanding its own central, constitutive practice, the Eucharist. The origins of the Lord's Supper must be complex, and undoubtedly different early Christian groups practiced and thought about it differently, though we know of no group lacking it altogether. On the other hand, as Paul Bradshaw has argued, the variety among the Synoptic Gospels may point to different understandings of the meal and particularly its association with Passover.[5]

The earliest attestation of the meal comes from Paul's discussion in 1 Corinthians 10–11. There he contrasts it with ritual meals associated with idols (1 Cor 10:14–22). He goes on to reeducate the Corinthians in the etiquette of the meal:

> For I received from the Lord what I transmitted to you: that the Lord Jesus, on the night he was handed over, took bread, and upon giving thanks, broke it and said, "This is my body on your behalf. Do this in my commemoration." Similarly, also the cup after they had feasted, saying, "This is the cup, the new covenant which is in my blood. Do this whenever you drink, in my commemoration." For whenever you eat this bread or drink this cup, you display the Lord's death until he comes. (1 Cor 11:23–26)

The education has several components: (1) a reminder of past conversations between the apostle and the church; (2) references to Jesus's actions; (3) quotations of Jesus in reference to the eucharistic meal; and (4) a commentary on the approved practice. Paul follows his usual practice of holding himself up as a model for his church's life (1 Cor 4:14–16; 1 Thess 2:1–12; cf. Col 1:24–29), but subordinates his teaching to that of God himself ("I received from the Lord"). Jesus's modeling becomes the ultimate touchstone of the Corinthians' practice because the crucified one is also available to them as the returning one.[6] Or, as Ernst Käsemann put it,

> The exalted Lord is and remains the Crucified, who calls his disciples to follow his earthly journey toward the cross. . . . The new world of the Body of Christ, while on earth still in competition with many other

5. Paul F. Bradshaw, *Eucharistic Origins* (Oxford: Oxford University Press, 2004), 8–10.

6. An elegant brief summary of Paul's position appears in Gerhard Delling, "Abendmahl II," *Theologische Realenzyklopädie* 1 (1993): 55–56 (47–58).

worlds and spheres of rule, is distinguished from them all by the *signum crucis* erected over it.[7]

For Paul, the Eucharist is part of an ecology of belief and practice that must be learned, and part of that learning occurs in the practice of the meal itself.

Over the church's history, there have been many discussions and the occasional knock-down-drag-out fight to make sense of the Eucharist and its relationship to the real presence of Christ, its status as a memorial, its proper administration, and so on. The most important discussion today must be the status of the Lord's Supper in a divided church and whether Christians in different bodies can rightly share in the meal without obscuring the real brokenness of the church. We cannot solve those significant issues in this book. It will require the prayers and actions of the whole church to do so.

Yet at the moment, a consideration of Paul's act of reeducation deserves attention. He rejects the agonistic, rivalrous view of communal meals that existed in the Corinthians' world. Far from being mere gatherings of friends celebrating the good things in life, the Eucharist signals the brokenness of a world that crucifies innocent people while also confessing the imminent end of that world as God breaks into it in the person of a Jewish man from Nazareth. To quote Käsemann again,

> We do not constitute that Body by entering into it as into an association. We are set sacramentally into that new world in which Christ is sole Lord even on earth, and the sacraments mediate a share in the crucified body of the exalted Lord, as Paul emphasizes with a singular acuity.[8]

The Eucharist in both Paul's world and ours is thus an exceedingly radical ritual moment, placing a giant question mark on all our perceptions of reality. Living between the horror of Golgotha and the splendor of the coming age, the church meets its Lord in the meal he instituted.

Part of the vocabulary of Paul's discussion in 1 Cor 11 is the word *anamnēsis* ("commemoration, memorial"). In the Greek Bible (the LXX)

---

7. Ernst Käsemann, *On Being a Disciple of the Crucified Nazarene: Unpublished Lectures and Sermons*, trans. Roy A. Harrisville (Grand Rapids: Eerdmans, 2010), 47.
8. Käsemann, *Disciple of the Crucified Nazarene*, 47.

the term appears relatively rarely but almost always in a ritual context. It can describe an offering that includes incense (Lev 24:7), apparently reminding God of Israel's needs and hopes. It can also describe the offerings made at Rosh Hashanah, reminding Israel in its celebrations of the good works of God (Num 10:10). And it appears in the superscriptions of two psalms (37 and 69 in the LXX = 38 and 70 in English and Hebrew). In both cases, the one being reminded seems to be God, who should act to save the petitioner from various distresses. The final instance of the word in the LXX occurs in Wisdom of Solomon, which speaks of salvation coming to those who have a "memory of the commandment of your law" (Wis 16:6). Here the one remembering is the pious human being, and the object of memory is Torah.

In the context of that usage, Paul's construal of the Eucharist as *anamnēsis* or reenactment takes on a different complexion. Of course, the rite cultivates human memory, orienting Christians to the core story of the faith, the unsettling story of Good Friday. Memory takes on the role of orienting the community to its own disoriented state, settles us into unsettledness, steadies us in the shakiness of the world of our experience. That much is clear. But does the Eucharist also remind God?

When Paul says we "display" Jesus's death until the Second Coming, to whom do we display it? Perhaps to the rest of the world, one might argue, but then again, the Eucharist in most Christian traditions has explicitly excluded unbaptized persons, and for good reasons. The meal is the place at which the community becomes itself as it enacts its story, its values, and its hopes. Perhaps to God? The Greek Old Testament's use of *anamnēsis* would support that possibility as would the much more common appeals to God to remember that appear in the Psalms and other liturgical texts.

This possibility has to be explored in much more detail than we can do here. If the Eucharist reminds not just the community but God of the death of Jesus, and if the reminder to God focuses on Jesus's sharing the fate of the innocent sufferer (as in Pss 37[38] and 69[70]), then the meal takes on powerful ritual resonances. The intended audience is God, as well as the human participants, as is true in all biblical (and many other) conceptions of ritual. If so, then the notion here is not far from the later development of understandings of Eucharist as a sacrifice. And if that is right, then the texts afford readers the opportunity to reconsider the link between sacrifice as a means of redemption and purification and the possibilities of education as formation for a meaningful, integrated life.

Sacrifice and Community Education

The cultivation of memory that occurs in rituals like Passover or the Eucharist depends on the sort of critical stance toward ritual that texts like Deuteronomy and 1 Corinthians assume. Both texts call upon human beings to reflect upon their practices and seek coherence between daily behaviors and the core commitments the rituals evoke.

Both the Deuteronomic circles and Paul (and other creators of texts now found in the Christian Bible) sought to reform and reconfigure traditional rituals in light of their understandings of the core values implicit within them. For Deuteronomy, that meant not just the elimination of deities other than YHWH from the Israelite community's worship, but a shift away from local sacrifices made in the context of family and village religion toward a more centralized approach in a temple that would serve as a symbol of the heavenly temple and so of the order of the cosmos itself. For Paul, the reform of ritual meant both the abandonment of the underlying polytheism of Greco-Roman culture and a renewed attention to the narrative behind the weekly ritual, Jesus's death on the cross.

In both instances, and others, the ritual reform harkened back to an underlying ritual practice, that of sacrifice. Sacrifice is *the* primal ritual, the one on which others depend for their meaning. Religion scholars have long debated the origins of sacrifice, and its earliest known purpose(s).[9] That topic is fascinating in its own right, but the Bible presents a set of reflections on sacrifice that not only long postdate the origins of the practice by millennia, but show so much reflection on it that its meaning can no longer be confined to its origins, whatever they were.[10]

9. Note, for example, the contributions in Robert G. Hamerton-Kelly, ed., *Violent Origins: Walter Burkert, René Girard, and Jonathan Z. Smith on Ritual Killing and Cultural Formation* (Stanford, CA: Stanford University Press, 1988).

10. For example, Burkert ("The Problem of Ritual Killing," in Hamerton-Kelly, ed., *Violent Origins*, 149–76) argues that sacrifice began with the hunt, which might be true since hunting and gathering predated agriculture, but in the Israelite tradition hunted animals could not legitimately appear on the altar, though they could figure on the household menu.

Those layers of reflection do not all agree in every detail, but they revolve around a few points:

- the management of violence
- substitution of a victim for the sinner
- communion among people and with God
- commemoration of past wonders constituting the worshiping community
- purification of the altar and sanctuary, and thereby the world

No single idea explains every detail of the Israelite sacrificial system or the Christian and Jewish processes of sublimating it within other religious practices. Just as "atonement" involves far more dimensions than substitution (contrary to many strands in fundamentalist Christian theology), sacrifice involves more than the removal of deliberate immoral acts.

An unusually instructive text comes in Leviticus 10 as part of the book's story of the creation of the sacrificial system in the tabernacle. This story marks the climax of a long section depicting the ideal sanctuary and the ways it should serve for worship that would purify the community and, in some ways, the world (Exod 25–Lev 10).

The inauguration of the sacrificial system began in chapter 9 with Aaron as the high priest carrying out the several sacrifices that would consecrate the people and remove the pollution of their sins from the altar in the tabernacle and therefore from the world. It then continues in chapter 10 with the work of Aaron's sons, Nadab and Abihu, who must be the first in a long line of priests carrying out the Israelite community's most important rituals.

The story introduces a terrible conundrum:

Aaron's sons, Nadab and Abihu, each took his censer and put fire in it. Then they put incense on it and brought strange fire before YHWH, which he had not commanded them. Fire [perhaps lightning] came down from YHWH's presence and consumed them. So, they died before YHWH, whereupon Moses said to Aaron, "That is what YHWH said, 'I will sanctify what is near me so that I will be honored before all the people.'" Then Aaron was silent. (Lev 10:1–3)

Without specifying the precise nature of the priests' infraction, the text makes clear its seriousness. The young men had violated a significant part of the ritual of sacrifice by deriving their fire from the wrong location. The error could hardly have resulted from ignorance or unclear instruction since Moses had taught them their duties in detail. It must have been deliberate or at least the result of carelessness.

The story may aim to explain why the priestly line of subsequent generations did not derive from the original clans of Nadab and Abihu. If so, the core of the story would serve a similar purpose to that of the story of the elimination of the Korahites and other clans from contention for the priestly office (see Num 16; but contrast the psalms of Korah). These narratives settle the question of who the legitimate priestly lines are.

Yet Leviticus 10 does much more work, including some literary tasks relevant to the question of teaching about and through ritual. The deaths of the young priests create the potential for crisis: a human corpse could defile the tabernacle and shut it down, so rendering the purification of the people much more difficult. Moses, therefore, steps in and orders his remaining nephews to carry out the work while others remove the charred remains of their brothers. He gives new instructions against the consumption of alcohol while on duty at the altar and orders the removal of the dead priests' bodies by members of the tabernacle staff. He also forbids mourning in the tabernacle itself during the period of sacrificing, since the logic of the dedication ritual demanded expressions of happiness in anticipation of successful worship for all future time.

The text, in any case, reflects in several other ways on ritual as a moment of instruction. The first comes in Moses's explanation of the prohibition of alcohol, which he calls an "eternal ordinance" whose purpose is "to distinguish between the holy and the profane, the polluted and the pure, in order to teach Israel's children the statutes that YHWH said to them via Moses" (Lev 10:9–11). The proper execution of the ritual involves a process of education through which the priests guide worshipers. The people must learn to identify things that are harmless in ordinary situations but out of place in worship, for a variety of reasons.

It seems odd at first glance to use the deaths of the priests as an opportunity to talk about the priestly teaching role, as Leviticus does. The logic seems to be that there are right and wrong ways to carry out a sacrifice, even with the relatively minor role ordinary people play in it.

A priest who plays the role intoxicated, much less one who flagrantly disrespects his work—all "his" in the ancient Israelite system—can hardly command respect from the worshiping community or properly lead them through the ritual. So, the sacrilege of Nadab and Abihu and their subsequent deaths provide an occasion for further instruction, not only in the world of the story but in the world of the reader who will visit the sanctuary to make such an offering.

The appearance of the same instruction (almost word for word) in Lev 14:57[11] and Ezek 44:23 is also instructive. The role of priest as a teacher of ritual distinctions occurs in the first case in the context of a discussion of skin diseases and their management, and in the second as part of a series of instructions for priestly conduct. The line must have been a well-known set-piece in the priestly educational system, a formula that could function in multiple settings but laid down a marker of the priestly identity as teachers (see also Deut 24:8; Mal 2:8).

The second pedagogical dimension of the story in Leviticus 10 comes near its end. Like their dead brothers, Eliezer and Ithamar failed to carry out the sacrifice properly. They incinerated the he-goat of the sin (or better, purification) offering (the *hatta't*), making it unavailable for human consumption (Lev 10:16). Their actions raised the question of what sort of *hatta't* was in play. The instruction for such an offering ordinarily involved the priests eating the meat as part of the ritual of purification. Ordinarily, they incinerated only the suet and the entrails, probably in the latter case to prevent their use in divination. An extraordinary *hatta't* that purified the sanctuary after a gross act of sacrilege demanded the incineration of the whole animal. The question then became which offering was to take place in this story, with Moses opting for the ordinary offering and Aaron for the extraordinary one.[12]

The young priests' mistake infuriated their uncle Moses, but their father Aaron rose to their defense with the argument that "today, they have brought their sin offering and their whole burnt offering before

---

11. The verb *yara* ("to teach") appears in Leviticus only in chapter 10 and at the end of chapter 14, which lays out procedures for managing skin diseases. The priests must "teach [the difference between] the day of impurity and the day of purity" (Lev 14:57).

12. See the helpful discussion in Jacob Milgrom, *Leviticus 1–16*, AB 3 (New York: Doubleday, 1991), 635–40.

YHWH, but these events [the deaths of Nadab and Abihu] have befallen me. Should I eat the sin offering today? Would that be a good thing in YHWH's view?" (Lev 10:19). Aaron makes the case that the offering must purify the sanctuary after such a calamity and that he and his surviving sons, who shared in responsibility for the problem created by the dead priests, should not benefit from their family's error in judgment.

The fact that Aaron makes an argument at all is instructive. Like Paul's discussion in 1 Corinthians 11, Leviticus 10 shows that the proper interpretation of a ritual as fundamental as sacrifice is subject to debate under at least some circumstances. The content of the argument is also interesting. For Aaron, the young priests have properly carried out the rituals because they took into account an intervening reality. The deaths of their brothers, Aaron's sons, rendered inappropriate the sort of celebratory atmosphere normally associated with sacrifice. The text acknowledges the humanity of those participating in the ritual even if it does not allow their natural and understandable grief and fear to shut down the sacrifice entirely.

Again, the argument works in the story world, describing an unrepeatable situation, the inauguration of the sacrificial system itself, and noting the potential danger present in even the most joy-filled rituals (much as the Eucharist recalls a judicial murder). But it also works in the readers' worlds, as they come to acknowledge the fact that even the most regimented, carefully circumscribed rituals take human experience into account even while shaping them in preferred directions.

In short, the final scene in this story serves an educational purpose. The various actors think through a dilemma possible in ritual when an event exposes a gap or a tension within the standard practice. They must work together to solve the dilemma and reach agreement on the solution.

The reader of the story can learn a broader lesson. Since most readers, even ancient ones, would never need to resolve a problem in the sacrificial system, the lesson must serve another purpose. It reveals at the very least the community's need to reflect on ritual, and it inspires reflection on the nature of reverence for God, respect for the dead, priestly service in times of crisis, and perhaps other topics. It shows a dynamic relationship between God and Israel in the persons of priests who must think about proper worship.

Prayer and Baptism

Sacrifice, of course, reveals many other aspects of human reality before God, and western Christians would do well to deepen our understanding of the practice as more than giving up something we like for a higher purpose. A more robust understanding would move us well beyond the overemphasis on substitutionary atonement as the only, or even primary, framework for understanding sacrifice. That deepening understanding would create space for liturgical reform so desperately needed, especially in evangelical churches. Unfortunately, we cannot take up that task here.[13]

We can say this: in ancient Israel sacrifice figured as part of a network of ritual practices, and those eventually absorbed it. In particular, prayer came to replace the offering of animals altogether while retaining some aspects of the theological reflections on the meaning of sacrifice. This move began certainly no later than the early Second Temple period, but matured after the Roman destruction of the Jerusalem temple in 70 CE suspended sacrifice as an available ritual practice. Christianity, as it separated from formative Judaism after the end of the first century CE, retained prayer along with key texts, beliefs, and practices.

Christians also modified a contemporary Jewish practice of ritual washing into a once-in-a-lifetime initiation rite, baptism. Baptism, in turn, sublimated concepts originating in the world of sacrifice. Both prayer and baptism have also served educational purposes that deserve further exploration.

Prayer. The observation that the church is a community of prayer seems a truism, honored if not always observed. Yet what is communal prayer in Scripture, and why does its recovery matter?

As the last work published in his lifetime, Dietrich Bonhoeffer wrote a pamphlet called the *Prayerbook of the Bible* about the book of Psalms. The Reich government censored the book for advocating the Christian use of the Jewish Bible, the Old Testament. Bonhoeffer rightly understood his work as part of the church struggle against National Socialism, a document of protest and a call to action.

13. A good discussion of sacrifice as a useful theological idea appears in Matthew Levering, *Sacrifice and Community: Jewish Offering and Christian Eucharist*, Illuminations: Theory and Religion (Oxford: Blackwell, 2005).

18

His tract begins with a reflection on Luke 11:1's notice that the disciples asked Jesus to teach them to pray. He remarks upon the counterintuitive nature of that prayer, at least for twentieth-century Protestants—and the same would be true now, more than eighty years later. The disciples' request seems odd to many modern Christians because we mistakenly think of prayer as deriving its meaning from a heartfelt longing to express ourselves to God, to empty out our innermost feelings in words directed upward. Yet, as Bonhoeffer says, "Praying certainly does not mean simply pouring out one's heart. It means, rather, finding the way to and speaking with God, whether the heart is full or empty. No one can do that on one's own. For that one needs Jesus Christ."[14] The Christological reading has its own history tracing back to the earliest stages of Christianity, and it shows an extraordinarily fertile imagination. To sing or speak the laments, hymns of praise, recitations of Israel's past, and paeans to wisdom as though in the company and under the guidance of Jesus of Nazareth surely opens the door to profound spiritual growth in the person so praying.

Yet here again, we are driven back to the same text Bonhoeffer began with, Luke's introduction to the Our Father and then to the prayer itself. The earliest readers of Luke, much less the disciples in the world of the story itself, would have recognized immediately the close relationship of Jesus's communal prayer to Jewish prayers of his era. Indeed, back-translating the text from Greek to an earlier Semitic (Hebrew or Aramaic) state requires very little scholarly imagination. The prayer bears the traces of its origins in most lines.

However, the intimate connections between this characteristic prayer of the early Jesus followers and the prayers of other Jews are a positive advantage to our understanding of prayer as a human activity that, in Bell's words again, marks "a way of acting that tends to promote the authority of forces deemed to derive from beyond the immediate situation."[15] Jesus in the gospels calls these "forces" "the kingdom of

14. Dietrich Bonhoeffer, *Prayerbook of the Bible: An Introduction to the Psalms*, ed. Gerhard Ludwig Müller, Albrecht Schönherr and Geffrey B. Kelly, trans. James H. Burtness, DBWE 5 (Minneapolis: Fortress, 1996), 155. We acknowledge, of course, the beauty and legitimacy of prayer in other traditions. Certainly, Christians can learn a great deal from the practices of prayer in Judaism and Islam. Here we focus, however, upon the church's life, not attempting to construct a broad theory of prayer.

15. Bell, *Ritual: Perspectives and Dimensions*, 82.

God/heaven." The Our Father bespeaks the early Jesus followers' radical take on the eschatological dimensions of Jesus's teaching.

In Luke's version, Jesus teaches the disciples to say,

> Father, let your name be sanctified;
> Let your kingdom come.
> Give us our day's bread each day,
> And lift our sins off us,
> Just as we do for all debts owed us.
> And do not lead us into trial.

The prayer was transmitted in a slightly different form in the community that employed the Gospel of Matthew, or at any rate the version in Matthew 6:9–13 shows some expansions that develop the main ideas of the prayer a bit further.

These expansions intensify or at least clarify the requests already present in the prayer. So, the hope that the kingdom will come gains greater depth with the request that God's will should find fulfillment on earth, among humans, just as it does in heaven, among the angels. The extraordinarily daunting request that humans will become as obedient and spiritually mature as their angelic counterparts sharpens the original request. Similarly, the expansion of the address from "Father" to "our Father in heaven" creates a more dynamic understanding of God as both intimately related to the praying community and radically transcendent of them.

Most to the point, both Luke and Matthew situate the prayer within a report of Jesus's educational interactions with his disciples. In Luke, the prayer comes at their request that he would "teach us to pray as John taught his disciples." Obviously, both sets of disciples had grown up in praying traditions within Judaism, which they did not abandon upon entering the fellowships of the two radical teachers. Quite to the contrary. The followers of Jesus adopted older practices wholesale, including the book of Psalms as a prayerbook. The Our Father itself fits squarely within Jewish ideas of the first century and long afterward, and it is difficult to see what in the prayer would have distinguished it from other Jewish prayers of the era except that Jesus taught it.

Matthew, meanwhile, situates the prayer in a discussion of acts of piety, especially almsgiving, and ends that part of the Sermon on the Mount (Matt 6:1–15) with a further clarification of the petition for forgiveness. Curiously, the gospel proposes to build a community marked by private, unostentatious prayer and acts of generosity. The members of that community will learn together to pray alone, will publicize concealment, and will celebrate obscurity. Windbags and charlatans need not apply.

The educational dimensions are at the forefront in both presentations of the Our Father, though in different ways. Yet one must ask what it means that the church has prayed such a penetrating, radical prayer daily, in many communal and private contexts, and in hundreds of languages for almost two millennia. The place of the prayer in Christian liturgies institutionalizes an apocalyptic mindset, preserving the earliest Jesus movement's sense that the present age cannot last forever. In each generation, the church learns to question its own perceptions of reality in light of its longing for the new reality that comes from God, the reality that Jesus called the kingdom.

Baptism. Baptism differs from prayer in being unrepeatable, occurring only once in a person's life. Yet it resembles prayer in other ways. Both prayer and baptism orient us toward a larger world beyond ourselves and empower the church to imagine itself living in that larger world. Baptism is a gift and invitation we receive rather than a work we do, as demonstrated by the fact that the person being baptized must submit to the experience.

Once again, the first person we know of to reflect on baptism as a window on moral or spiritual formation was the apostle Paul. As part of his exploration of how human beings, both Jews and Gentiles, receive divine mercy through faith, he takes up the question of how we escape the power of sin. In other words, he traces the effects of the cross, especially for those who trust God as the giver of salvation. He writes,

> What shall we say? Should we remain in sin so that grace may abound?
> Of course not. How can we who have died to sin live in it anymore?
> Do you not know that whoever has been baptized into Christ Jesus has
> been baptized into his death? Therefore, we have been buried with him
> through baptism into death, so that just as Christ was raised from the
> dead through the Father's glory, we also might walk in a new sort of
> life. For if we were planted together in the similitude of his death, we
> will similarly be in his resurrection. Knowing this, that our old person
> was crucified so that the sinful body might be destroyed, so we might
> no longer serve sin. (For the one who dies is justified from sin.) But if

we have died with Christ, we believe that we will also live with him, knowing that since Christ was raised from the dead he is no longer dead, and death no longer dominates him. For whoever has died, has died to sin once, but whoever lives, lives for God. So also, you should consider yourselves dead with respect to sin but alive with respect to God in Christ Jesus. (Rom 6:1–11)

The somewhat convoluted prose deals with many issues in Pauline theology as the apostle picks his way through a thicket of problems. But three key points stand out.

First, Paul sees a parallel between the believer's experience of baptism and Jesus's death and resurrection. Baptism imitates the core Christian story and inducts the one trusting in God into the entire divine economy of mercy and grace.

Second, this induction into grace also marks a liberation from the power of sin and death, a complete break from the enslavement of the superhuman forces of evil that preclude human flourishing and render life painful and futile.

Third, and most importantly for the present discussion, Paul thinks that reflection by already-baptized persons upon their own baptism will deepen their trust in God, their self-awareness, and their capacity for moral decision-making (see Rom 12:3–21). He encourages the Romans to "consider yourselves dead with respect to sin but alive with respect to God." That is, they no longer live as slaves of sin, subject to its compulsions and pain. They live in the realm of God.

Peter Stuhlmacher understands Paul in this text to be defending himself from charges of preaching cheap grace, among other things.[16] Paul tries to situate the mission to the Gentiles within the ongoing story of Israel and God, and this has led him to place limits on the efficacy of Torah without, however, abandoning it. He threads a very small needle, but he does thread it, and the fabric he sews together clothes the community he tries to form. That community fully embraces the story of redemption, even keeping Torah after a fashion (Rom 13:8–14). It does not understand its righteousness as precondition of salvation, but as salvation's consequence.

---

16. Peter Stuhlmacher, *Biblical Theology of the New Testament*, trans. Daniel P. Bailey and Jostein Ådna (Grand Rapids: Eerdmans, 2018), 386.

In some parts of the early church, adults on the verge of baptism often stripped off their clothes and entered the font naked. After their immersion, they emerged from the water to put on new clothes. This ritual symbolized their entrance into a new life. They put on Christ after casting off the works of sin and death. The initiation ritual touched ordinary life and transformed it.

A church planter acquaintance of ours has asked those becoming Christian in his congregation to do something similar, though more appropriate to contemporary culture. Adults about to receive baptism wear clothes symbolizing their old life into the baptistry, and then change into new clothes outside it. In perhaps the most dramatic example, a woman who worked as an exotic dancer wore her old outfit one last time, surrendering it to her new Lord.

Another friend borrowed that idea for his own congregation, asking new Christians to surrender some symbol of their old life. One man brought his *Merck Manual* to throw it away. It had been his Bible for mixing illegal drugs in meth labs and similar haunts for many years. The years of dealing death and misery gave way to a new life.

These creative retrievals of the ancient practice allowed converts to the faith to enact the apostolic observation, "We, therefore, were buried with him through baptism into death, so that just as Christ was raised from the dead through the Father's glory, so we also should conduct ourselves in a new way of life" (Rom 6:4). Creative teachers found ways to concretize high theology while marking major changes in the lives of real persons.

Stories like these from the contemporary church are legion, and they deserve more press and more reflection than they usually receive or than we can give them here. They illustrate the power and the opportunity of creative engagement with the Christian tradition by those who claim it as their own faith. They remind us that the imagined world of the popular consumerist culture need not be the world in which we live. Many other options exist.

Ritual, Reflection, and Formation

At this point, an attentive reader should wonder whether we have not introduced a contradiction into our thinking. If, as Rappaport argues, ritual is "the performance of a more or less invariant sequence of formal acts and utterances not entirely encoded by the performers,"[17] then it becomes difficult to speak of the ideas transmitted by ritual. In truth, many contemporary scholars of ritual have adopted a largely "practice-oriented" approach that keeps theological reflection at bay. Rappaport's language is carefully chosen at this point, however. The meaning of ritual is not "entirely" encoded by the performers. That is, ritual embeds layers of meaning that accrue over time, defy easy linguistic analysis or expression, and persist in spite of efforts at innovation.

To put this more clearly, when Paul invites his readers to consider the implications of the Eucharist or baptism for their lives, or when the Pentateuch invites laypeople to celebrate the festivals, they do not assume that the meaning of the event will depend upon the ruminations of participants in the moment. There is something to the ritual practice in time and space that depends on prior performances and the possibility of continued performance for its meaning. The community must be formed not only to carry out the specified actions accurately, but to reflect upon their implications for life even outside the ritual moment.

This point takes us back to Bell's description of ritual as "a way of acting that tends to promote the authority of forces deemed to derive from beyond the immediate situation."[18] Both Jewish and Christian rituals point participants to the realm of the divine, where God, the angels, and humans interact around the deep wisdom of the cosmos. The movements of bodies in space, in interaction with each other, etches on the participants' consciousness an awareness of something lying at the edge of human language or just beyond it. If we could put all of that into words, we would not need ritual. If we could put none of it into words, then it would not be the subject of formation or education.

Ritual, then, points to mystery. While the biblical story allows a community of faith to plot its place in the world and consider the merits and demerits of behaviors and life patterns, ritual in the church both actualizes story in its life and signals to it that it cannot narrate its own story without reference to the divine. When priests or pastors proclaim the bread of the Eucharist to be the body of Christ, following the words of institution of Jesus himself, they are not primarily entering into a discussion about the nature of the bread (the hoary debate about the

---

17. Rappaport, *Ritual and Religion*, 24.
18. Bell, *Ritual: Perspectives and Dimensions*, 82.

"real presence"). They are yet again inviting a community into a way of life full of divine wonder.

Since the Protestant Reformation, Christians have debated the number, nature, and frequency of administration of sacramental acts. The debates have often masked a deeper agreement on the need to mark important transitions in life (birth, marriage, parenting, death) with communal ritual bespeaking "the authority of forces deemed to derive from beyond the immediate situation."[19] Repeatedly, the revitalization of ritual has led to the revitalization of the church. Eucharistic congresses have recalled Catholics to regular patterns of confession and prayer, for example. In some cases, the emphasis on ritual has underwritten a rediscovery of the church's story.[20] And while Protestants have often sought revival through preaching, the ritual element has never been far away.[21] Pentecostalism has emphasized ritual acts (usually not eucharistic), often while insisting on the free movement of the Holy Spirit in human behavior (which seems very stereotyped to an outside observer, fitting the definition of ritual we are following here). Our point is not to pass judgment on the theological merits of these myriad activities but to note the phenomenon. Ritual renewal has always been an important element of church renewal.

On Teaching Ritual

As the old boundaries between ecclesial families become ever more porous, some ritual practices are taking root in places previously inhospitable to them. One of the most powerful is *lectio divina*,[22] the slow, devoted, and prayerful reading of Scripture. This ritual practice invites not primarily close analysis of a text, but surprise and wonder. It requires

---

19. Bell, *Ritual: Perspectives and Dimensions*, 82.

20. As argued by Ann Morrow Heekin, "Christian Story as Ritual Engagement: The American Liturgical Renewal in the Rise of Narrative Theology," *Proceedings of the 2006 Meeting of the Religious Education Association*, https://old.religiouseducation.net /member/06_rea_papers/Heekin_%20Ann.pdf (accessed 13 March 2023).

21. See, for example, the discussion in Ann Taves, *Fits, Trances, & Visions: Experiencing Religion and Explaining Experience from Wesley to James* (Princeton: Princeton University Press, 1999).

22. See in detail, John Westerhoff, *Spiritual Life: The Foundation for Preaching and Teaching* (Louisville: Westminster John Knox, 1994).

the creation of space in which the teacher recedes to allow the students to speak. Other practices include breath prayers or the repetition of the Jesus Prayer ("Lord Jesus Christ, Son of God, have mercy on me") or a quiet listening process in which one prays with the prophet Samuel, "Speak, Lord, your servant is listening" (1 Sam 3:10). These psychosomatic practices from Eastern Orthodoxy point to a profound desire to adore God and so escape sin's power exercised through the senses.

The list is long, in fact, as the modern world of ubiquitous communication makes available to searchers within and outside the church a range of possibilities. That ubiquity creates the problem of eclecticism and even voyeurism, as searchers piece together behaviors that seem attractive without much reflection on the theological grounding of any of them. For many US churches, steeped in pragmatism, defining "what works" will present serious challenges not quickly answerable. This is particularly true in denominations and congregational networks that lack theologically vigorous and informed teaching offices. Creating space for prayerful reading during communal worship will benefit the participants in it.

The Wild West of options presents opportunities for teaching, however. Ritual practice within a community follows patterns, often centuries old, so that the wisdom of the past and the needs (not merely fads) of the present can match. Ritual practice evokes, provokes, and convokes. In celebrating the Eucharist or praying together whether in the words of Scripture or some other words, the church evokes the ecology of grace of which it is part and to which it points. The words of Scripture, in particular, because of their often-jarring contrast with present-day assumptions about reality, disrupt the patterns of life scripted by capitalistic accumulation, consumption, and display. Consistent ritual practice also provokes reflection about the moral commitments of participants (If we recall the exodus, can we oppress migrants? If we recall Golgotha can we pursue unbridled self-interest?). And ritual convokes a community committed to the world to which the ritual points.

Ann Grodzins Gold describes her experiences in trying to teach about rituals as actions in the material world to students who largely wish to focus on ideas. In particular, she invites students to describe their own traditions, complete with ritual objects (crucifixes, *tefillin*) and theological ideas about the meaning of the practices. She observes that many practitioners of ritual, in many religious traditions, will claim that the ritual does not work by itself but only at the prompting of the divine realm. Baptism does not save *ex opere operato*, just as bathing in the Ganges does not bring purity. Yet participants in the rituals take them with great seriousness on the conviction that they do somehow contribute to the desired outcome of lifting the human person out of the brokenness of the world into something higher. She notes especially how students study pilgrimage rites in different traditions as a way of understanding what religions share in common and how they differ.[23]

We are not focusing here on teaching comparative ritual, but on helping Christians lean into the practices of their faith. But Gold has put her finger on important elements of teaching through ritual. We must engage in ritual and then reflect on what we do. For example, the weekly practice of the Lord's Supper, if done thoughtfully and prayerfully, would create space for just such a back-and-forth process. We also need wise guides for that endeavor. And we need to associate the rituals with living human beings, the Swankies of the world, whose need for wholeness echoes our own.

23. Ann Grodzins Gold, "Still Liminal after All These Years: Teaching Ordeals and Peregrinations," in *Teaching Ritual*, ed. Catherine Bell (Oxford: Oxford University Press, 2007), 29–44.

CHAPTER 5

Prophecy and Prophetic Christian Formation

If ritual texts seem slightly alien to some modern western Christians, especially those who have learned from the Protestant Reformation to be suspicious of ritual, then even more alien are those texts that come under the label "prophetic." Ancient Christians might remember the prophets of Israel as models to be emulated, but their successors today have great difficulty making sense of Isaiah, Jeremiah, Ezekiel, or the Twelve Minor Prophets. This is true for several reasons: the texts themselves are highly complex compositions; they ask radical, unsettling questions about how human society should function; and their answers do not look much like bourgeois Christian viewpoints.

In this chapter, we attempt to lay out how the shaping of the prophetic books fed a tradition's ongoing imagination as well as the need to speak of both tradition and imagination. We then turn to a case in point, parts of the book of Amos. Amos's rich texture models a prophetic discourse addressing the community of faith's life in the world. We next probe the role of poetry in the prophets and the church's ongoing encounter with the prophetic books. And finally, we try to delineate the scope of biblical prophetic books as they sketch out alternative worlds and name ways to teach that vision in the church's life.

From Divine Pathos to Tradition

A number of years ago, Walter Brueggemann wrote an important little book called *The Prophetic Imagination*.[1] He opened with the claim

---

1. Walter Brueggemann, *The Prophetic Imagination*, 2nd ed. (Minneapolis: Fortress, 2001).

that "the contemporary American church is so largely enculturated to the American ethos of consumerism that it has little power to believe or act."[2] He blames that state of affairs on "a depreciation of memory and a ridicule of hope" in favor of an obsession with the moment. All of that indictment—or cry from the heart—rings true. It has certainly become even clearer in the aftermath of a global pandemic in which many churches were nexuses for wild-eyed conspiracy theories and irrational behaviors. Many Christians experienced the loss of comfort and economic progress as a loss of hope in God. In too many cases, the core Christian story had gone missing amid the bluster of nationalism and love of ignorance.

At the same time, we can go further than Brueggemann did, in important ways. It seems fairly clear that in today's church we have nothing less than a conflict between a truly Christian view of the human self and a modern, bourgeois one. In the latter, the human is primarily a consumer and producer, a person whose radical freedom of choice centers upon objects and experiences created by business and checked, legitimately or otherwise, only by the laws of an increasingly disrespected state and what remains of personal ethics. In the former, by contrast, human beings live as partners in God's creative work, pursuing just and merciful lives. They treasure the creation as a gift not just a resource. They see not just signs of sin everywhere, but also tokens of grace. They live in a God-saturated world.

Brueggemann goes on to argue for an alternative, a recovery of the church's hope and memory. He maps the modern western mixture of consumption and the pursuit of power onto the ancient Israelite "royal consciousness," which he understands as a betrayal of the radicalism of Moses and his legacy.[3] The solution to the church's problem comes from a recovery of the prophet's critique of the structures of power and their "embrace of pathos," that is, their sense of the reality of human suffering and the need to name it, to weep with those who weep as well as rejoicing with those who rejoice. The recovery of pathos leads, in turn, to a renewed energy and a sense of amazement at the work of God.

The second edition of Brueggemann's book ends with reflections on the connection between prophetic imagination and ministerial practice.

2. Brueggemann, *Prophetic Imagination*, 1.
3. Brueggemann, *Prophetic Imagination*, 21–38.

For him, the latter means primarily work that highlights the realities of poverty and oppression even within the rich nations of the world. He concludes by noting that the relationship of imagination and practice is "a defining one for the church that will become more crucial and more difficult, and perhaps more joyous, in time to come."[4]

Brueggemann's little book has prompted many other works, not just from his own pen as he amplified (and indeed, recycled and repeated) his ideas further but as others especially in ministerial practice developed them as a way of radically rethinking their work outside the parameters of church administration, preaching, and leadership previously taught as the arts of ministry in many seminaries. The boundary-crossing and paradigm-shattering nature of his proposal has been visible, and its influence has largely been helpful. We ourselves owe him a debt for our own thinking.

At the same time, however, quite a few problems of both fact and interpretation make Brueggemann's approach less helpful than it might seem at first. It is not simply that his emphasis on Jesus as a foil to establishmentarian religion risks feeding the very anti-Jewish Christian supersessionism Brueggemann rightly deplores,[5] or that his sharp contrast between the royal and non-royal views in ancient Israel oversimplifies the historical complexity, or even that "imagination" is a very complex phenomenon. (And very creative, imaginative proposals for human life can be profoundly evil. We have to ask about the content of imagination.) The real problem is that the prophetic books work differently than Brueggemann's model assumes, since they do not simply capture free imagination but channel it into a tradition.

Scholarship on the Israelite prophetic books has moved a great deal in the past few decades. There has been a growing awareness, for instance, of the care with which the four prophetic books (Isaiah, Jeremiah, Ezekiel, and the Twelve Minor Prophets) were put together. Relatedly, the consciousness of individual prophets or what Abraham Joshua Heschel spoke of as "a fellowship with the feelings of God, a sympathy with the divine pathos," an idea to which Brueggemann was

---

4. Brueggemann, *Prophetic Imagination*, 125.
5. Jon D. Levenson, "Is Brueggemann Really a Pluralist?" *Harvard Theological Review* 93 (2000): 265–94.

heavily indebted, has become far less central.[6] Perhaps the current scholarship has overreacted and over-focused on the bookishness of the prophetic legacy. But the realization of the literary nature of prophecy offers important insights for contemporary reflection.

Imagination and Tradition

Part of the issue we face is how we understand the intersection of tradition and imagination. One of the legacies of the Enlightenment of the eighteenth century is a tendency to understand tradition as a drag on human flourishing, a fancy way of masking unearned privilege and power. Another countervailing trend inherited from Romanticism (itself a reaction to the sterility of much of the Enlightenment project) is the return to tradition as an aesthetic, a sort of game that people play for their own enjoyment and enrichment, or as a protest against the emptiness of late capitalism and the commercialization of every aspect of life.

Obviously, we are painting with a very broad brush here. However, neither of these approaches to tradition seems fully satisfactory. It turns out that the pursuit of pure reason obliterates a great many wonderful aspects of human existence and tends to promote the values of elites in the West at the expense of almost all the rest of the human race. On the other hand, a sentimental view of tradition does not carry much water either.

The prophets, to return to the case at hand, come down to us in texts carefully arranged, edited, and preserved by a succession of their students and admirers. Over one hundred generations of readers have mulled over their words, attempting to hear through them (and through prior reflections on them) words that say something true about God's work in the world. The careful curating of those words must have some meaning. The fact that the disruptive, disorienting poems have reoriented people matters. What do we make of the reality that we read these texts in the company of many others who may not share our assumptions, interests, or values in full?

The prophetic books take up multiple ideas and images, but their work seems to revolve around three major topics. First, they reflect on the ways of YHWH in the human world, including the massive historical

6. Abraham J. Heschel, *The Prophets* (New York: Harper & Row, 1962), 26.

changes that befell Israel and Judah during the mid-first millennium BCE during the period of forced migrations. Their field of vision extends far beyond the spiritual lives of individuals or small groups to a region-wide (or from an ancient perspective, worldwide) perspective. Second, they play upon their own language, as newer prophetic texts rethink the implications of older ones. And third, they feed conversations about alternative worlds in which, as Amos 5:15 puts it, the people of God "hate evil and love good, and carry out righteousness in the gate" (i.e., courtroom).

The Ways of God in Human Existence

The prophets of ancient Israel ended up as teachers of a sort. The collection and dissemination and revision of their words provided language for generations of Jews, and then Jews and Christians, to try to make sense of their own experiences. Those acts of "making sense" have donned many guises, from calculators of the timetable of the second coming to sophisticated cultural critics. That history of interpretation is in itself a fascinating tale.

Yet here we should focus more tightly on how the ancient texts themselves examine the world. A previous generation of scholars often talked about the ways of God in history (in contrast to myth, usually), though the prophets themselves had no word for such an abstract enterprise as "history." They reflected on the events they saw unfolding around them and created new ways of seeing the world, often challenging the dominant discourses either of the empire invading them (as with Isaiah's use of Assyrian propaganda against itself) or of the more local machinations of elites known to them (like Jeremiah's critiques of the priest Pashhur or Amos's of Jeroboam II and his minions). They are hard to peg on a political spectrum, ancient or modern.

Their conceptions of divine or human activity require examination. Unlike many modern Christians since the early 1600s, the Israelite prophets believed in divine activity on large and small scales.[7] They were not credulous: they asked questions about God's activity and denied

7. On "atheism" as a catchall term for various forms of questioning traditional religion, see Alec Ryrie, "Reformation," in *The Cambridge History of Atheism*, ed. Stephen Bullivant and Michael Ruse (Cambridge: Cambridge University Press, 2021), 183–201; and his larger book, *Unbelievers: An Emotional History of Doubt* (Cambridge: Harvard University Press, 2019).

some claims about it, as when Jeremiah repudiated the prophets who expected a quick return from Babylonia for the forced migrants (Jer 28–29). At the same time, they did not think God had retired to a condo in Florida next door to Santa Claus and the tooth fairy.

Take the book of Amos, for example. The namesake prophet lived in the eighth century BCE, a period of significant political change throughout western Asia and the eastern Mediterranean. The Assyrian Empire began its century-long ascendancy, bringing to an end more than a dozen smaller states and fostering a trading regime that extended from Spain to Afghanistan and beyond. Amos lived on the cusp of an era that would see the destruction of his primary work environment, the northern kingdom of Israel, and the forced removal of parts of its population. The difficulties of the future lay just beyond him. The book, because it was edited in the generations after him, reflects both the ongoing turbulence of the whole Assyrian period (and probably later) and his own time as well.

What sort of book is it, and how does it foster reflection on the work of God among humans? How does it tradition imagination, so to speak?

A good example of imagination drawing on and reinforcing tradition occurs in the complicated set of poems in Amos 5. Following the critique of many nations in chapters 1–2, chapters 3–6 turn the prophet's fire upon Israel proper. Found within this longer section of the book, chapter 5's cluster of short utterances begins,

> Hear this word, which I am raising against you, a lament, O house of Israel.
> "Fallen, Virgin Israel won't rise again,
>   left from her land, no chance for her to get back up."
> For thus says YHWH the Lord,
> "The city going forth a thousand will have a hundred left,
> and the one going forth a hundred will have ten left—for the house of Israel." (Amos 5:1–3)

This bleak estimation of the future, probably the people's immediate future during a time of war against an irresistible empire, is attributed to the deity. As such it bears the stamp of inevitability, of authority.

Yet even the bald words raise problems. On the one hand, the reference to the people through the feminized term "Virgin Israel" raises the question of their final status. Is the label ironic? Does it signal the vulnerability of women during a war of conquest, when rape is a real threat and often a matter of policy rather than happenstance? Does it name the vulnerability of all the people? Or perhaps the label's ambiguity is deliberate as the audience must ask what it means.

On the other hand, the seeming finality of "won't rise again," which later parts of this same cluster of poems will modify and even contradict, raises the question of the speaker's attitude toward the event. Does God relish the people's destruction or lament it? The answer is not clear as yet.

The text continues, then, with another oracle formula and a complex combination of indictment and invitation:

> For thus says YHWH to the house of Israel,
> "Seek me and live.
>> Do not seek Bethel
> or go to Gilgal
>> or travel to Beersheba.
> For Gilgal will surely be forced to migrate
>> and Bethel will be for iniquity."
> So seek YHWH and live,
>> lest he intrude into Joseph's house like fire
>> and it devours and nothing can quench it for Bethel. (vv. 4–6)

This exhortation complicates the audience's understanding of its own tradition, devaluing traditional rituals and holy sites (Bethel, Gilgal), not in an absolute sense, but in order to recast their purpose.

Pilgrimage to already ancient sites serves many purposes for worshipers, reminding them of the stories and practices of their ancestors and connecting them to the divine realm. This is still true today for many who travel to Mecca, Jerusalem, Rome, or other places like Santiago de Compostela. The ancient site creates a space for meaning-making. To disrupt or question the legitimacy of pilgrimage in the name of a purer piety, as Amos does, requires an alternative. It is not clear how sharp a contrast the text means to pose between "seeking Bethel" and "seeking YHWH." While a text like 1 Kings, influenced by Deuteronomy's notion of a single national sanctuary, might pose an absolute sort of distinction—YHWH cannot be found in Bethel—the book of Amos on the whole seems to take a less extreme position. Still, something about the traditional practice requires change.

The cluster of poems proceeds to such an alternative, beginning in Amos 5:14, but not before prefacing it in several ways. The first step in the reconstruction of traditional practices comes in the appeal to other traditional language, the hymnic fragment in verses 7–8. It contrasts

> Those turning justice into wormwood
> > and dumping loyalty onto the ground

with

> The One making the Pleiades and Orion,
> > the one turning darkness into morning,
> > darkening day into night,
> the one calling to the sea's waters
> > and pouring them on the ground—
> YHWH is his name. (vv. 7–8)

The astronomical abilities of the creator God come to the fore in this fragment of a hymn. This language is part of the Israelite tradition, and to some degree was inherited from the religious discourses of the ancient Near East. But why does it appear here?

Earlier scholars sometimes thought of verses 8–9 especially as an intrusion into the argument, though this understanding does not really account for why someone would add it. The more interesting approach would be to ask how it interacts with the poems around it. The hymn shows up here as a way of decentering the human experience for the all too human readers. The focus shifts from the corruption of the legal apparatus, the cruelty and corruption of the courtroom, to the world beyond the discourses of justice and meaning, to the world of the stars and the passage of days and seasons.

By jamming this hymn in between two indictments of Israel's injustice (verses 7 and 10–13), the text delays the inevitable conclusion of its argument (a device that gives the hearer a bit of a break from the ferocity of the prophetic criticism). More importantly, however, the hymn shifts the focus from the human side of pilgrimage and courtrooms, the places in which people gather to do the business of the community, toward a view of the world in which such arenas of human behavior come to seem very small and short-lived in comparison with the patterns of the cosmos that set the landscape on which humans move about. In view of our smallness, how should we behave?

The rest of the chapter turns first to indictment and then to appeal, interweaving the two sorts of language to create, again, a complex dialogue within and among the readers as they—we—must decide upon the nature of our own agency.

> They hate the one reproving in the gate,
>> abominate the one speaking the right things. (v. 10)

Their emotional and intellectual disposition prejudices them against justice, and in turn it throws everything out of kilter. Therefore, their mansions (v. 11, "houses of ashlar construction") will be abandoned and their well-cultivated vineyards abandoned. These images are both shorthand for the massive disruption that resulted from the Assyrian invasions and their subsequent rearrangement of the economy of Israel and its neighbors.

The prophetic text proposes a view of causality here. The injustices of some of the people and their disregard for the rights of others would lead to a society-wide meltdown and would prompt foreign invasion and conquest. Perhaps a modern reader would draw the lines of cause and effect somewhat differently, but as a text from a colonized people, the book of Amos seeks at once to reclaim agency for the people and to frame their work in a much bigger setting far beyond human control. This mental somersault becomes the basic move of all the prophetic tradition and in many ways the basis for later Jewish and Christian reflection on the morality of communities and nations. Much is at stake here.

Toward the end, the text returns to traditional language, which it modifies and subverts without replacing. This happens in several stages. Verses 18–20 question the wisdom of seeking "YHWH's Day," apparently already by then a traditional label for a day of divine intervention on behalf of the people. Amos accepts the idea that such a dramatic intervention will occur and that it will be executed justly and to the benefit of the just. But he flatly and ominously denies that his audience form part of the just who may reasonably long for such a judgment day. Quite the opposite. YHWH's intervention will be a tragedy for them.

The cluster of poems ends with a prophylactic, a call to agency that is also a wish for an alternative. It comes packaged as divine indignation at worship practices that seem blithely indifferent to the suffering of people.

> I hate, I reject your festivals,
>> I do not enjoy your assemblies.
> Your incinerated offerings won't reach me,
>> nor will I accept your gifts,
> nor will I look at your fatty reconciliation offerings.
> Get the din of your songs from me.
>> I won't listen to the music of your lyres. (vv. 21–23)

Again, the text has turned back to—and turned its back on—traditional religion and in particular its major practice, sacrifice, the purpose of which was to link God and Israel into a relationship of mutual gift exchange. Sacrifice united the divine ruler with the human subjects in a relationship of honor and benefaction. To repudiate those practices risks obliterating that world of mutual obligation, an act that could not have aided the very ones to whose suffering Amos calls attention.

The unsatisfactory nature of this disorienting call—unsatisfying because it solves little—can only be remedied by a human embrace of agency, which nevertheless does not rely simply upon human policies or concrete actions. Rather, the prophetic vision moves to the world of imagination:

> But let justice roll along like water
>> and loyalty like a perpetual stream. (v. 24)

This move does not leave tradition or collective memory behind altogether, since the prophet turns at last to query the audience's understanding of their own history, asking whether sacrifice graced their original relationship in the desert and expecting a negative answer. The rituals, while important and valuable, cannot ground their relationship with God. That relationship can only ground the rituals.

Yet this line does much more than call its hearers to alter their course. The combination of the nouns *mishpat* and *tsedaqah*, "justice" and "loyalty," appears earlier in verse 7, with which verse 24 forms an inclusio, an envelope into which other images are stuffed. The words themselves could be translated in several ways, with varying degrees of abstraction ("justice" and "righteousness," the commonplace translations, may be too vague or too abstract). They denote the legal situation in which vulnerable people receive proper defenses in the local courts, but also the underlying attitude of equity and fair play that can make a justice system viable or, if absent, the opposite.

Here Amos does more than call for the opposite of the present reality. Not only does the text not specify what the alternative world should look like, it moves the discussion of due process and fair outcomes to the poetical world of bodies of water, "perpetual streams." Powerful people should not be able to turn off the tap of justice whenever they wish. Caprice and special interest ought never to prevail.

There is more to this poetic turn. The first word of verse 24, *wey-iggal* ("and let it roll along"), circles back to the more complex pun of verse 5 *haggilgal galoh yigleh* ("Gilgal will surely be forced to migrate"), again forming part of the envelope with the early part of the chapter. The pun is mostly lost in an English translation but not to the original hearers, surely.

Still, the word play raises more questions than answers. Can a sudden conversion to justice-making avert the forced migrations, which came as a result of Assyrian foreign policy and the miscalculations of the Israelite elite (see 2 Kgs 17)? The forced migrations resulted in all sorts of unjust acts and gratuitous suffering. Could a culture that pursued justice for its members have avoided such a tragedy? The word play cannot answer those questions, but it can trigger them, forcing a new sort of discourse whose failure to provide neat and tidy answers is itself a sort of answer. The community reading this text must evaluate its own practices, values, and beliefs and begin to discuss alternatives.

Much of this text is familiar ground to students of the Old Testament, of course. It is often, and rightly, taught in introductory classes as an antidote to the pursuit of comfort characterizing much of the church in anglophone North America (and well beyond). Amos swings a scythe through middle class complacency and domesticated theology.

Yet even scythes cut grain for harvest, and ultimately for the nourishment of the farmer and the farmer's family and community. The disorientation and critique must be part of something larger. This is especially true for the modern readers. The theological work of the past two generations has thoroughly cut the established church down to size. Its current fragmentation and shrinkage surely call for something else. The 1960s were a long time ago. How should we hear and teach such a text?

Many citizens of the United States, and now others, will hear Amos's words in the voice of Martin Luther King Jr., who quoted the prophet in his justly famous speech at the Lincoln Memorial on August 28, 1963. King's quotation comes as part of a response to those "who are asking the devotees of civil rights, when will you be satisfied?" Against calls for a truce in the war for civil rights, a truce advertised under the name of moderation and love of the common good, King insists, "We are not satisfied," when a long set of undesirable conditions exist:

> We can never be satisfied as long as the Negro is the victim of the unspeakable horrors of police brutality.
> We can never be satisfied as long as our bodies, heavy with the fatigue of travel, cannot gain lodging in the motels of the highways and the hotels of the cities.
> We cannot be satisfied as long as the Negro's basic mobility is from a smaller ghetto to a larger one. We can never be satisfied as long as our children are stripped of their selfhood and robbed of their dignity by signs stating: for whites only.
> We cannot be satisfied as long as a Negro in Mississippi cannot vote and a Negro in New York believes he has nothing for which to vote.

The images cascade in a way that an Amos would have appreciated, concretizing specific sites of injustice without limiting the analysis to those evils.

King's use of anaphora concludes with the response to the white moderates, the unreliable allies for whom the appearance of justice is more important than the reality. King says,

> No, no, we are not satisfied, and we will not be satisfied until justice rolls down like waters, and righteousness like a mighty stream.[8]

---

8. https://www.youtube.com/watch?v=smEqnnklfYs&t=926s. The text appears in Paul Finkelman and Bruce A. Lesh, eds., *Milestone Documents in American History*, 4 vols. (Dallas: Schlager, 2008), 4:1752–54.

Many of his original audience would have recognized the quotation of Amos 5:24 at least as biblical even if they could not necessarily give book, chapter, and verse. Contemporary audiences might well mistakenly attribute the final image to the speaker, whose life as a Baptist preacher steeped in the cadences of the Bible has fallen into the background in a more overtly secular society.

King's speech has become part of the canon of American mass culture, and so its radical nature has often gotten lost. Even prophets can be commodified and domesticated by a culture bent on doing so. The words deserve a new hearing, however.

By placing Amos's words in the context of the discontent of those who seek justice, King invites his hearers into an ancient tradition that should take them back behind the founders of the country, whose heritage he seeks simultaneously to receive, critique, and modify. This more ancient tradition, that of the Israelite prophets and the minority of readers who embraced their words, taps into the unarguable sanctity of the divine, and by appropriating it, King and his audience place themselves on the side of justice not only in an abstract sense but in tangible, measurable actions. In a sense, this contextualization of Amos is an improvement on the original.

On the other hand, the use of King's speech in a more secular context raises many questions for the interpreter of the Bible. How do we connect the political with the religious, the immediate with the transcendent, the messy and contingent with the eternal? King's use of Amos may help revivify the ancient words, but it may also obscure them or replace them. Reappropriation of texts always runs that risk. A text like this invites modern readers to rethink our use of sacred space and the stories we tell about it, leading us to rethink what we mean by the "sacred" itself.

The text of Amos disrupts its readers' complacency. It does so by rethinking space and the way a community inhabits it through its rituals and judicial structures. Sites of pilgrimage can only serve their intended purposes if the community accepts the applicability of its story of the divine and, in particular, of YHWH's justice to the courtroom and the workspace. Those inhabiting such reimagined space collaborate with YHWH in fashioning a way of life that stands as perpetual objection to other ways of life.

Willie James Jennings, reflecting on Bishop Colenso, the nineteenth-century Anglican leader in KwaZulu-Natal, notes that the leader began his career deeply enmeshed in the colonialist agenda of the British government and church. Over time, however, he came to listen to his Zulu interlocutors and so to challenge the white European reading of the Bible and understanding of Christian theology and Christian space. As Jennings puts it,

> The theological implications of Christian translation were often concealed to the colonialist translator. The story of Israel connected to Jesus can crack open a life so that others, strangers, even colonized strangers begin to seep inside and create cultural alienation for the translator and, even more, deep desire for those who speak native words. These implications are far greater than emancipatory possibilities for indigenes rooted in vernacular Christian agency or budding cultural nationalisms, but in joining—loving, caring, intimate joining. That joining is a sharing in the pain, plight, and life of one another.[9]

Jennings's description of the process through which the Christian story can transform both the oppressed and their allies ("translators") is not far from what happens in the encounter between the prophetic text of Amos and its generations of readers, early or late. The words of the biblical text and the claims to which they point "crack open a life." The words signal the validity of the experiences of colonized persons (whether the ancient Israelites or nineteenth-century Zulus or others) such that readers taking the words seriously must question comfortable assumptions about their relationships to other people. The critique of power becomes a lament for the loss of intimacy among human beings. It also becomes an invitation to a new sort of life.

The Poetry of Prophecy

The encounter between text and reader happens in different ways with the prophetic books since the books differ from each other. They share in common, however, a poetic sensibility, and in our reflections on

---

9. Willie James Jennings, *The Christian Imagination: Theology and the Origins of Race* (New Haven: Yale University Press, 2010), 165.

teaching and learning them, it is important to ask what difference it makes that they are primarily, though not exclusively, collections of poetry.[10]

In modern US society, poetry often lacks the prestige it has earned in other settings. Poets of protest like Wendell Berry or singers like Pete Seeger or Bob Dylan may gain culture-wide recognition, but the popularity of a few masks the marginalization of the many. Certainly, in ancient cultures, poets were honored even when their poems challenged convention or offended the powerful. Many living cultures share the same attitude, especially when poetry functions to commemorate a present or past in danger of being suppressed or forgotten. As the Russian poet and victim of the Stalinist terror, Nadezhda Mandelstam, said, "If nothing else is left, one must scream. Silence is the real crime against humanity."[11]

Unfortunately, anyone trying to read poetry in the contemporary church in the United States must overcome the prejudice in many quarters that the entire enterprise bears the stamp of elitism or decadence. Our deeply pragmatic culture makes only one exception, poetry set to music, sometimes rewarding the creators of banal or even crass lyrics with millions of dollars and celebrity. We face, in other words, a distorted sense of values. The church will help its cause by inviting the poets into its walls as members or at least honored guests. Texts like Johnny Cash's "When the Man Comes to Town" or Maya Angelou's *I Know Why the Caged Bird Sings* point to the horrors of the world and the possibility of redemption, and invite a further encounter with the biblical text. Perhaps the closest parallel to biblical prophecy appears

---

10. Isaiah includes some prose narrative (Isa 36–39), Jeremiah much more, and Ezekiel also a great deal. Even that material, however, works in a highly elevated way to tell the story of the prophets in question and to situate their words in a larger context. Significant scholarship has emerged on the literary purposes of these prose texts and their relationship to the poetry with which they intertwine, beginning, notably with the work of Ernest W. Nicholson, *Preaching to the Exiles: A Study of the Prose Tradition in the Book of Jeremiah* (Oxford: Blackwell, 1970). For a fine reading of Isaiah's poetry, see J. Blake Couey, *Reading the Poetry of First Isaiah: The Most Perfect Model of the Prophetic Poetry* (Oxford: Oxford University Press, 2015).

11. Nadezhda Mandelstam, *Hope Against Hope: A Memoir*, trans. Max Hayward (New York: Atheneum, 1970), 43.

in slam poetry or hip-hop, forms that play with the riches of language to provoke, invoke, and evoke.

But to return to poetry as a medium of communication, we ask why the Israelite prophets and even such early Christian successors as the author of the book of Revelation resorted to poetry. The prestige of the medium must have been a significant motivation. However, there must be more at stake, in part because the prophetic books themselves, when they foreground the prophet's biography, present their hero as a marginalized figure on the outs with the power structures or the people as a whole (for example, Jer 18:18–23; 20:7–18; Amos 7:10–17). Prestige works in complex ways.

Perhaps a larger consideration goes to some of the characteristics of poetry itself. Without trying to propose a theory of Israelite poetry, much less poetry more generally, it is safe to say that poetry has certain features that lend themselves to prophetic speech. The condensation of ideas into relatively few words or images leads to memorability, obviously an advantage in communicating the texts to audiences over time. Those same qualities can also produce shock or delight in ways that prose forms struggle to do.

Perhaps an even more significant feature is the mimetic quality of poetry. In a study of the poetry of Charles Wright, Helen Vendler describes his work as refusing "mimesis of the external world (sea, dirt, weather); mimesis of the psychological world (name, dreams, face); and mimesis of the religious world (attendance, consolation, help)." To give up so much, she insists, means that "many of the tones that we associate with poetry must be forgone."[12] On the one hand, for Vendler, "we" have come to expect poetry to imitate life in its multiple dimensions. On the other, it need not always do so, and the varying degrees of austerity and self-discipline a poet may exercise may derive from the refusal to imitate life or allow the words to open up worlds beyond themselves.

How might such a view apply to the biblical prophets? A great deal. The poems in Isaiah, Jeremiah, Ezekiel, and the Twelve Minor Prophets show varying degrees of mimetic sensibility, everything from the imitation of sounds *ka-thunk ka-thunk* (*tsav letsav. . .qav leqav*; Isa 28:13) to images like Zeph 3:17's

---

12. Helen Vendler, *The Ocean, the Bird and the Scholar: Essays on Poets and Poetry* (Cambridge: Harvard University Press, 2015), 63.

YHWH your God is among you, a heroic rescuer.

He sings over you with joy, revels in his love, celebrates over you with a shout.

The divine opera singer with Israel's restoration as the theme of his song signals more than a timetable for the trip back home from Mesopotamia.

The myriad images employed by the prophets have occasioned many studies in biblical scholarship, and some excellent surveys of biblical poetry exist.[13] It is also increasingly clear that we need to attend to the way these texts present themselves as spoken words, deliberately creating the appearance of orality for an audience that must listen and respond.[14] There is no need to rehearse all of that work here. However, one important insight does deserve reflection. Dobbs-Allsopp notes the brevity of most biblical poems (and this applies to the prophets), their concentration into what we like to call lyric (as opposed to epic) poetry. As he puts it,

> Lyric, as I have said, is typically short, enacted on a small scale. Only so much can be accomplished in a language art that routinely foregoes [sic] the use of cohesion-aiding devices, such as plot, argument, or consistency of character.[15]

That description applies to most prophetic texts constituent of the major prophetic books, though the combination of the texts may constitute a sort of argument or plot (and much more work on that question remains to be done by biblical scholarship). The limited scope of the texts explains both their power and the frustration many of their readers feel. Power, because the texts evoke a much larger world than they can fully imitate. Frustration—and possibly delight—because the gap between text and world calls for constant reinterpretation in which readers may never reach a full consensus.

13. Most notably, F. W. Dobbs-Allsopp, *On Biblical Poetry* (Oxford: Oxford University Press, 2015); more briefly, Elaine T. James, *An Invitation to Biblical Poetry* (Oxford: Oxford University Press, 2022).

14. The work that Jacqueline Vayntrub has done for other poetic texts surely applies to the prophets as well. See her book, *Beyond Orality: Biblical Poetry on Its Own Terms* (New York: Routledge, 2020), esp. 9–11.

15. Dobbs-Allsopp, *On Biblical Poetry*, 214–15.

But back to Vendler and the biblical prophets for a moment. Her tripartite understanding of the objects of mimesis—the natural world, the psychological world, the religious world—sheds some light on our encounter with the prophetic books of the Hebrew Bible. These texts relish the reality of the world of stars and plants and animals, that is, their power, beauty, and sometimes horror. They also explore the dynamics of human life, though without the modern hard distinction between the "real" interior of the person and the outward "performance" of that person within community. They do without that sort of understanding, preferring to see human beings in relationship. Still, an exchange like

> A voice says, "Cry out."
> And I say, "What shall I cry?" (Isa 40:6)

already opens up the possibility of a distance between the prophet and the reader by signaling the existence of both. The answer to the query, "All flesh is grass," doubles down on the identification since the readers must now either deny the obvious truth of the statement or accept their own provisional nature, the frailty of human life itself, the limits of understanding and meaning-making.

Mimesis extends also, as Vendler insists, to the religious world, which of course is the prophets' forte. They would undoubtedly quibble with her gloss of "religion" as "attendance, consolation, help," since the God they characterize does not always offer consolation except by the most indirect route. Rather, they see God's help as awaiting a human response and finding none (except the creation of the very texts that signal human failure), acting to save anyway.

This latter move underlies many biblical texts. The very structure of each book of the Twelve Minor Prophets builds in this plot point, for each book ends with some version of a hope oracle for Israel (even if that hope involves the defeat of enemies as in Nahum). Some of these feel tacked on, as when Amos shifts from "Behold, YHWH's eyes are upon the sinful kingdom, and I will destroy it" (Amos 9:8) to "In that day, I will raise up the fallen booth of David" (Amos 9:11), ushering in a new era of abundance and peace. Others are more integral to the book's plotting, such as Hosea's image of renewal in which both Israel and YHWH became verdant plants in a world of justice (Hos 14:1–8

[2–9]) or YHWH's final plaintive question in Jonah (4:11), "Shall I not have regard for Nineveh?"

Either way, the shift is built into the larger books as well, as when Ezekiel ends with an extended vision of a renewed temple fit for the majesty of Israel's God (Ezek 40–48) or the Third Isaiah insists that "YHWH's hand is not too short to rescue, nor his ear too heavy to listen" (Isa 59:1). The prophetic books do not see the tension between divine justice and divine mercy as ever fully resolvable in favor of one attribute or the other. Rather, these seemingly opposite qualities appear throughout almost as two poles of the same battery, with each necessary for the activation of the other. The poetry must always cycle in on itself because human existence before God always returns to its beginning point, though never by the same route.

Alternative Worlds?

These features of the biblical prophetic text raise for anyone reading or teaching them an important question. What is the scope of these texts? How big is their imaginative world?

In a word, big. A half century ago, the New Testament scholar Ernst Käsemann observed that, "today more than ever faith must develop reason and imagination." He signaled the helplessness of practical reason (the can-do attitude of the western world) "against the mechanisms, apparatuses, and forces of the economy, technology, and social and political conditions."[16] This need is all the greater today when nationalism is again on the march, and artificial intelligence threatens to alter the very definition of human creativity. What would a renewal of the church's imagination, especially one conditioned by the prophetic texts of the Bible, look like?

To return to an earlier part of this chapter, we began by noting the value of imagination in Christian theological reflection, particularly reflection on the meaning of the biblical text. We also argued that the sort of imagination matters, and that sort is deeply conditioned by the shape of the texts themselves and by the church's practices of reading

16. Ernst Käsemann, *Church Conflicts: The Cross, Apocalyptic, and Political Resistance*, ed. R. O. Siggelkow, trans. Roy A. Harrisville, foreword by James H. Cone (Grand Rapids: Baker Academic, 2021), 143. The original German essay from which this quote comes dates to 1972.

our Scriptures, and the prophets in particular. We have also noted the limits of those texts, which deliberately choose to work on small canvases and then display them in the same exhibition hall in order to create something greater than the sum of the parts. That sum marks the scope of their imagination.

To be plainer, the four biblical prophetic collections, as well as the book of Revelation, all understand the world they are imitating and evoking to include divine actors (true and false, YHWH and rivals), human beings from both the Israelite kingdoms and foreign states, and plants and animals. They see the "real" world as a highly dynamic place under divine control, without absolute clarity about the mechanisms of that control. Some of the world must remain inscrutable.

The Israelite prophets understand the world to be populated with a single divine actor, YHWH, the God who freed Israel in the exodus and interacts with its rulers and others through prophets. The heavens and the earth were the stage upon which YHWH acted or remained still, depending on the needs of the moment. Along with YHWH were of course the people of Israel and the nations. Each prophetic book thinks about both, concentrating primarily upon either Israel or Judah, and often blending the peoples of the two states into a single entity, but also offering "oracles against the nations" (Isa 13–23; Jer 46–51; Ezek 25–32; Amos 1–2). These complex texts show a variety of viewpoints on, and levels of information about, neighboring powers.

Why does an attention to the scope of prophecy matter for its interpretation? Sometimes we poll our students on the question, "What is your understanding of prophecy or prophetic communication?" Their answers tend to fall into three categories: prophecy as prediction of the messiah and the transformation of the world through him; prophecy as social critique, as the call for social justice; and prophecy as a lived experience giving wisdom to the church and its members today. These views are not logically exclusive, and plenty of Christians espouse a combination of some version of two or even three of them. They do, however, have different pedigrees, the first from premodern Christian readings, the second from liberal Protestantism and the African American church, and the third from Pentecostalism. In the contemporary mix of popular theologies that exists in almost all churches, it is useful to understand the histories and current permutations of these understandings of prophecy.

The point we make here is not to try to solve this problem or take "sides" in a potential debate, but simply to ask what the biblical texts saw as the scope of their art and what that understanding might mean to their readers today. To answer that question, it is relevant to note, again, that the creators of the great prophetic collections in the Old Testament (Isaiah, Jeremiah, Ezekiel, and the Twelve Minor Prophets), as well as Revelation in the New Testament, situated their oracles and stories on a very large landscape populated by God, divine messengers such as the seraphim, Israelite leaders and commoners, and foreigners of various ranks. The landscape was also thickly settled by non-sentient beings whose decline or revival mirrored, and often stood in for, the experiences of humans.

Reading those works, then, requires close attention and creativity. In her study of stories of sexual violence against women in the Hebrew Bible, Rhiannon Graybill considers the case of "Daughter Zion," a literary figure created primarily by the prophets as a way of exploring the horrors of the mass deportations of the eighth–sixth centuries BCE. The great Mesopotamian Empires (Assyria and Babylonia) and, to a lesser extent, the even greater Persian Empire used forced migration as a tool of rule. This character "Daughter Zion" became a way of exploring the horror, trying to locate causes and effects and, if possible, to find a path toward repair. The character works in various ways, many very unpleasant, in order to explore the generalized violence befalling many citizens of Israel and Judah during the period in question, and in order to signal that at least some of the violence was sexualized.[17]

As Graybill notes, the texts about this character are almost unique in the Bible in their willingness to explore the aftermath of sexual violence. This is especially true in Hosea and Ezekiel (Hos 2; Ezek 16; 23).[18] Graybill queries approaches to these texts that understand Zion as an innocent victim (quite contrary to the stated views of the texts themselves). She does not want "her" ("Zion") to be simply a victim, arguing that "interpreting in sympathy with or on behalf of can also mean speaking in place of."[19]

17. Rhiannon Graybill, *Texts after Terror: Rape, Sexual Violence, and the Hebrew Bible* (Oxford: Oxford University Press, 2021), esp. 113–43.

18. Graybill, *Texts after Terror*, 113.

19. Graybill, *Texts after Terror*, 121.

Instead, turning especially to the book of Lamentations, Graybill asks us to think of Zion's resilience or "grit," her determination to survive even when the ultimate perpetrator of the violence against her is YHWH. Attention to the high level of artistry of Lamentations might either sharpen or diminish the pain of the character and the reader, an ambiguity that calls upon all the skills a reader may have available. Careful readings that acknowledge complexity of the text and the reader's stance toward it can open the door to a range of interpretations and a rich dialogue.

Graybill's case study has broader implications for reading the biblical prophets, for those texts invite a range of responses. We might consider an example to illustrate this need.

The first comes from the introductory chapters of Jeremiah. The unremitting criticism of chapters 1–6, in particular, seems hard to take. The prophetic voice scores the people and their leaders for injustice, leaving no room for a solution. Typical are such indictments as

> For from the least of them to the greatest of them,
>> everyone is avaricious,
> From prophet to priest,
>> everyone lies.
> They have doctored my people's wound carelessly
>> by saying, "Peace, peace"—
>> but there is no peace. (Jer 6:13–14)

Or again,

> Cut your hair and toss it away,
>> Then raise a lament on the bare heights,
> for YHWH has repudiated and rejected
>> the generation irritating him. (Jer 7:29)

The former example highlights the disruption of social norms, including the role of the prophet and priest as teachers and moral standard-bearers. The latter takes the story a step further, just past the moment of invasion and destruction, as the people mourn the horror of the experience. In the first, the tragedy comes about through the misdeeds of people, in the second, through the actions of God.

Texts like these—and the whole book of Jeremiah with its almost unrelieved language of terror (one of Jeremiah's favorite words, incidentally)—trigger many possible reactions. Some readers will simply take the indictment at face value, joining in the piling on without either recognizing their own sins or dealing with the collateral damage of the events the texts describe. Other readers will find the indictments to be unreasonable, with YHWH playing the role of a tyrant or rapist of a people. Both approaches are easy to document in the scholarly and popular literature.

Graybill's approach, to which we broadly subscribe, offers a more productive path, and that path appears in the texts themselves. Alongside the excoriating language of Jeremiah lurks another voice. The prophetic persona in Jeremiah also speaks about exasperation and doubt. (We do not enter into the question of how exactly the words of the text relate to the words of the prophet whose name the text wears.) This voice says such things as

> To whom shall I speak and bear witness so that they will listen?
>> Their ears are uncircumcised,
>> so they can't pay attention.
> YHWH's word was something shameful to them.
>> They did not enjoy it.
> I keep speaking about YHWH's wrath,
>> I cannot hold it in.
> Pour it out on children in the plaza,
>> on the mob of young people together. (Jer 6:10–11b)

Texts like this, which recur in Jeremiah, state a discomfort with the divine word and its repercussions, even while leaving God's accountability latent rather than explicit.

That voice goes further in the book, however, in a text like Jer 8:18–9:6. Here the prophet, speaking either for YHWH or for himself, says,

> My smile gone, grief over me,
>> my heart sick. (Jer 8:18)
> The reasons lie close at hand:

> I am shattered over the shattering of the Daughter of My People.
>> I mourn. Shame has overpowered me.

> Is there no balm in Gilead,
> > no doctor there?
> For why has not the healing of the Daughter of My People come about?
> (Jer 8:21–22)

Many aspects of that snippet of text are instructive. It frames the prophet's reaction as a question, expressing the dismay and consternation of an observant person responding to the tragedy of forced migration and its aftermath as perpetrated by Nebuchadnezzar and his state. The question invites reflection on human and divine agency and empathy for human suffering, even when the prophet believes it is warranted by the evil deeds of those very people.

There is also a strong sense here of the personal trauma befalling the literary character the book calls "Jeremiah," whatever his relationship to the living person. This character can speak of bewilderment. He can also speak of outrage directed against God, not only for imposing on him an offensive, miserable mission (Jer 20:14–18; cf. 1:4–10), but also for disrupting the whole universe in order to inspire a sense of justice in the elect people.

This takes us back, then, to the question of the scope of the prophets. Jeremiah exemplifies an extraordinarily complex set of attitudes toward his own people, the events they experienced, the prophetic role, and the stance of God toward humans and vice versa. That honest discourse, that exploration of the emotional life as well as the bare facts of political and military history, reveals a multidimensional world about which the prophetic books speak.

That literary world embraces the whole world available to humans, blurring our sharp distinctions between public and private, economic and familial, and religious and secular. The sheer comprehensiveness of the prophetic vision challenges our theological reflection on the world, providing raw material for moral reflection and worship.

On Biblical Prophecy and Prophetic Teaching

How might the church engage the biblical prophets in ways that bring forward their vision of the world in new situations? Or put differently, how can the prophetic tradition live today? The prophetic texts occupy a quarter of the Bible, yet many churches never read them much less study them with awareness of their aims or techniques of communication. Recovering their voice is highly desirable.

These texts point to at least four areas in which the church might grow in its practices. The first is liberation of the oppressed. The prophetic texts draw readers into the messiness of history and politics as they impinge on ordinary people's lives. The texts identify the possibilities and the limits of the agency humans might experience based on their social status and social capital. The sober analysis of injustice that appears in Amos or Jeremiah, or indeed most of the prophetic works, paves the way for an equally detailed analysis of injustices in our own setting. This is a zone of inquiry in which the social sciences and history have much to offer the church, in company with a close reading of Scripture. When the church reads a summons like "Let justice roll down like waters and righteousness like a mighty stream" (Amos 5:24), it must either reject the call or think hard about its implications for our behaviors as an identifiable community.

The second area shows up in concrete spiritual practices. Later prophetic texts underscore the keeping of Sabbath, for instance (Isa 56:4, 6; 58:13–14). A robust life of prayer is characteristic of prophetic texts, inasmuch as they assume the divine presence amid all their workings. The deep work of spiritual growth has often figured in liberationist movements drawing on the prophets, and there is no particular reason to play the two modes of life off against each other. As Howard Thurman put it in a sermon once, "What I do in the moment of prayer is merely the creative synthesis of what I do always. And the pressure, the relentless pressure, is on me to live so that I desire to withhold nothing from Him [i.e., God]—to let His life and His love and His scrutiny play over the stuff of my days."[20] For Thurman, the spiritual life equaled the prophetic life, as an awareness of the worth of the human being before God transformed individuals, groups, and societies.

The third area concerns the role of human beings as those who listen to God. The prophetic books are often couched as divine speech with phrases such as "thus says YHWH" or "an oracle of YHWH," indicating the perspicacity of the texts themselves as they both invigorate life and "remain forever" (Isa 40:7–8; 55:10–11). For example, Jeremiah uses the word šāmaʿ ("to listen, hear") about 180 times, often in the plural

---

20. Howard Thurman, *The Growing Edge* (New York: Harper & Brothers, 1956), 53.

(Jer 2:4; 7:2, 23; 10:1; 11:2, 4, 7; 13:15; 17:20; 19:3; 21:11; 26:13; 29:20; 31:10; 42:15; 44:24, 26). Normally, the call to listen introduces some sort of warning, a call for change. Jeremiah's notion of divine kingship includes the idea of YHWH as a speaker, much as is true of the other prophets. The audience of a given text is listening not just to it, but to God. This is not simply a bid for power on the texts' part. It is a call for the audience to imagine itself in a different world than the one it perceives otherwise.

The fourth area centers on ideas of hope. To teach and learn the prophetic texts is to cultivate the practice of hope, an attitude closely related to the reality of liberation. The prophetic texts do not merely offer social critique. They invite their hearers to imagine alternatives and to begin practicing those alternatives in their daily interactions. A church that takes them seriously would find partners in the pursuit of social justice in order to remedy the ills of their community. It would also plumb the depths of its worship of God as a way of exploring alternative views of human life in God's created and creative world. The poetry of prophecy asks us to imitate a world we have not yet fully entered.

In her discussion of catechesis, Anne Marie Mongoven turns to the importance of symbols of revelation, including Scripture. Understanding symbols as things that point to other things, in this case to God's self-revelation, she frames the task of formation this way:

> The goal of symbolic catechesis is to strengthen the faith of the catechetical community and each member within it. No one can program an experience of God nor growth in faith. Those are grace-filled moments. But the catechist can bring together the community and the community's symbols in such a way that the community recognizes the extraordinary character of its own life.[21]

Mongoven's understanding of catechesis applies to a broad swathe of practices, but it applies to the specific challenges of teaching and learning the biblical prophetic texts in particular. The prophets point toward the world of God, which ultimately lies beyond human control or even comprehension. Teaching such texts must evoke that world, and this means teachers cannot focus overmuch on either methods or

---

21. Anne Marie Mongoven, *The Prophetic Spirit of Catechesis: How We Share the Fire in Our Hearts* (New York: Paulist, 2000), 111.

consequences. Teaching these texts should help the church enter the same sense of wonder the texts themselves bespeak.

Mongoven's last phrase is telling: the church recognizes "the extraordinary character of its own life." The imaginative community begins to see possibilities in the mutual support of its members and in their interactions with others in God's name.

CHAPTER 6

Wisdom and Its Cultivation

Wisdom and its acquisition have probably always exercised human beings. As sentient beings who wonder about all the things around us and can examine our own thoughts and thoughts about our thoughts, we naturally wish to live in ways that are prudential and virtuous. Although the perceived content of wisdom and methods of its acquisition vary across cultures and eras, a surprising number of commonalities also exist. The pursuit of wisdom lies at the heart of the teachings of the Bible and therefore the religious traditions that claim it as Scripture. How, then, do the biblical texts speak to such a persistent reality?

This question is more acute today because of the unique realities of our world. The explosion of data over the past few decades has made the discovery of wisdom harder, not easier. At least some estimates predict that human beings will soon produce 463 exabytes of data (463,000,000,000,000,000,000 bytes) *per day*. Those same estimates guess that human oral communication over the past 100,000 years might come to about *twenty minutes'* worth of that production. Even allowing for the facts that we do not know how talkative our Neolithic ancestors were, and that most communication is nonverbal, it is easy to see that we are in a completely different world of information production and sharing than any previous generation.

It is also clear that much (virtually all) of this ocean of information is too trivial to contribute to the accumulation of wisdom. The endless details of consumer preferences may make some people wealthy, but they do not enrich our minds or souls. Some of this mountain of data serves sinister purposes—think Russian troll farms and QAnon and the chaos sown on social media. Quantifying the percentage of the trivial and the evil is probably not possible since the categories depend on prior ideas about wise and unwise, as well as good and evil. But perhaps we can agree on the broad strokes: the pursuit of wisdom is desirable, and it is uniquely hard in our time because of the surfeit of information that does not help, and often hinders, that pursuit.

In our turbulent environment, nothing could be easier or less helpful than simply to inveigh against the follies of the age, however. The critique of culture has a long history in Christian responses to modernity, sometimes producing unhelpful sour verbiage. That sourness is not our preferred flavor profile, however. We want something different.

We might begin by acknowledging the presence of some good news in this brave new world. Even with the overwhelming presence of the media culture and its relentless attempt to commodify experience and sell every aspect of life to the highest bidder, it is not hard to find people who live differently. Sometimes that difference appears in counter-communities that embrace older ways of living, whether as comprehensive lifestyle or as part of a mix of practices. These alternatives might focus on more modest consumption or the recovery of lost methods of production. Or they may attend to social relationships in healthier ways. Alternative communities have popped up in many religious traditions, from the Catholic monastic orders to the Hutterite colonies. Far more people are grabbing bits and pieces of older practices and ideas in order to fashion a meaningful life free from the dictates of the advertising-industrial complex. That creative search for meaning where it can be found seems most promising.

In our time when many of us do seek wisdom, we argue that the biblical wisdom texts furnish both models of learning and content for that learning. Here we introduce the idea of wisdom as a practice, delineate some of the ways the biblical wisdom texts build that practice, and offer two case studies (Job and the Sermon on the Mount) before drawing conclusions about the place of wisdom texts and the pursuit of wisdom in the church.

Wisdom as a Practice

Contemporary scholars currently debate whether a distinct wisdom "tradition" existed in ancient Israel, and if so, of what it consisted.[1]

---

1. For example, see Mark Sneed, ed., *Is There a Wisdom Tradition? New Prospects in Israelite Wisdom Studies*, Ancient Israel and Its Literature 23 (Atlanta: SBL, 2015); Will Kynes, *An Obituary for "Wisdom Literature": The Birth, Death, and Intertextual*

Theologies of the Old Testament/Hebrew Bible have notoriously struggled to find ways to incorporate the texts defined as "wisdom texts" into their overall structure. At the same time, it is clear that some texts lack the emphasis on Israel's distinctive narrative characteristic of most of the rest of the Bible. Wisdom texts do not present themselves as stemming from prophets or storytellers, and the liturgical needs of the priesthood do not interest them. So, it is reasonable to think of them as different, whatever their origins.

These texts include, most obviously, Proverbs, Ecclesiastes, and Job. In the extended Christian canon, Ecclesiasticus (Sirach) and Wisdom of Solomon also figure, as do James and parts of the gospels and epistles. These texts, though they differ among themselves and originate over several centuries, share in common a focus on the string of proverbs as a meaningful unit of communication. The pursuit of prudential living led to literary genres that took advantage of the localized nature of truth and the limits of human capacities to understand and act upon that localized truth. The string of aphorisms may be fairly short, as in most of the book of Proverbs. Alternatively, the string may develop into a fairly long discourse that owes a debt to other literary genres, as when Job also draws heavily on the sorts of liturgical texts evidenced in the book of Psalms. In both cases, however, close observation of the small details of life build a larger picture.

These texts also share some key ideas (to which we will return) and a basic conviction of the availability of wisdom to all human beings. They draw heavily on the conventions of ancient Near Eastern thought, though their cosmopolitanism does not lead them to repudiate the unusual features of Israelite thinking. Most importantly, they do not embrace polytheism, even if they do accept notions of creation similar to the theologies of some of Israel's neighbors (for instance, Job 38:4–41 has many parallels to other, non-Israelite texts). They pursue prudential living while maintaining a complex relationship to traditional religious practices or beliefs.

The wisdom texts can be extended further in the Christian canon to include some psalms (Pss 1; 19; 49; 112; 119; 128). The New Testament also

---

Reintegration of a Biblical Corpus (Oxford: Oxford University Press, 2019); and earlier the proposals of Leo Perdue, *Reconstructing Biblical Theology: After the Collapse of History, Overtures to Biblical Theology* (Minneapolis: Fortress, 2005).

contains texts resembling collections of Proverbs, such as the Sermon on the Mount (Matt 5–7), the closely related Sermon on the Plain (Luke 6:17–49), and the Epistle of James. One might argue that the parenetic sections concluding each of the Pauline and post-Pauline epistles and even 1 John are "wisdom" texts.

It is also noteworthy that ancient Jewish thinkers often conflated Torah with wisdom, and if we follow their lead, then the category becomes very expansive indeed.[2] This conflation began in the biblical period itself, because the chains of proverbs and the chains of laws follow a similar pattern of organization. The scribes copying both kinds of texts organized them similarly.[3] However, the more thorough merger of the genres came later. Judaism has always thought of the Torah (the Pentateuch) as more central than Proverbs, Job, or Ecclesiastes, but all these texts and the halakhic texts that interpret the laws of the Pentateuch reflect the deepest sort of wisdom. As the conclusion of the book of Sirach put it around 200 BCE, accepting the yoke of Torah will allow a person seeking wisdom to find the proper education (*paideia*) (Sir 51:26). Then, that person may "rejoice in God's mercy" and, by pursuing wisdom with resolve, will find that God will "give your wage in its time" (Sir 51:29–30). That intertwining of Torah, prayer, properly oriented affections, and trust in God constitutes wisdom for a text like Sirach and for later Judaism and Christianity.

What the book of Sirach describes is wisdom not as a body of fixed ideas or data, but as a process (or cluster of processes) of learning. Wisdom is a practice, an art to be cultivated. In making such an assertion, it is also important to clarify what we mean by the word "practice." In ordinary English, the noun "practice" may denote an event in which those engaging in something rehearse the work they will do later in earnest, often under the tutelage of an experienced teacher. When our children were young, we took them often to "piano practice" or "basketball practice," for example. Another meaning, perhaps more basic,

2. See the discussion in John Collins, "Wisdom and Torah," in *Pedagogy in Ancient Judaism and Early Christianity*, ed. Karina Martin Hogan, Matthew Goff, and Emma Wasserman (Atlanta: Society of Biblical Literature, 2017), 59–79.

3. Eckart Otto, "Weisheitliche Proverbienredaktion und ihre Amalgamierung mit keilschriftrechtlicher Redaktionstechnik in den Sammlungen kasuistischer Rechtssätze im biblischen Recht," *Zeitschrift für die alttestamentliche Wissenschaft* 134 (2022): 458–82.

is what the *Oxford English Dictionary* describes as "the carrying out or exercise of a profession, esp. that of medicine or law." This meaning goes back to the fifteenth century and underlies much of what this chapter means by "practice." The *OED* also notes another relevant meaning, "The actual application or use of an idea, belief, or method, as opposed to the theory or principles of it; performance, execution, achievement; working, operation; (*Philosophy*) activity or action considered as being the realization of or in contrast to theory." That meaning also dates to the fifteenth century but is not what we mean by the term. We do not wish to pose a hard split between "theory" and "practice" but to think of them as inextricably intertwined.

Back to the first two meanings, then. Common American English usage speaks of an experience in which persons "practice" (the verb now) a skill in order to get better at it. The missed notes on the piano or bad passes on the basketball court, when examined and corrected, can lead to a better performance later. The teacher or coach suggests or shows ways to improve the performance, and the learner tries again until things improve. The good teacher can help the learner become more self-aware and find a voice, a way of inhabiting the activity being learned. A bad teacher may impart all the right technical lessons but destroy the student's desire to continue. The art of teaching and the art of learning go together.

This first usage of the word "practice" leads quickly to the second, "the carrying out or exercise of a profession." In his study of how people acquire expertise, Roger Kneebone speaks of developing a voice. For example, the bespoke tailor learns to copy the masters perfectly before striking out in a new direction with a distinctive style, even while always retaining the skilled practices of cutting and sewing. Or again, the surgeon must cut precisely in order to bring health, while also perhaps innovating new techniques that work even better. "Voice," he says, "shapes how you navigate the space between you and whoever you are with."[4] That is, learning a practice involves many sorts of skills, attitudes, values, and relationships acquired over time through the tutelage of more advanced practitioners, as well as one's own efforts. This

4. Roger Kneebone, *Expert: Understanding the Path to Mastery* (London: Viking, 2020), 205.

combination of actions and attitudes behind them is close to what the biblical texts call "wisdom."

Kneebone adds many other layers to his conception of how we become experts, at least one of which is directly relevant to the study and teaching of the biblical texts. Part of a practice is its inherent unpredictability or risk-taking. Even the virtuoso pianist may miss a note. A hall-of-fame-caliber athlete may miss a short jumper, even one that would have won a championship. Unlike a 3D printer, which fashions exactly what it is told to, a sculptor may find the chisel slipping at just the wrong spot, but may also adapt that mistake to a higher purpose. Kneebone again: "Experts take responsibility for the variation inherent in their work. They read the materials they work with and the people their work is for. . . ."[5] Again, this is part of what the Bible calls "wisdom."

It happens that the biblical texts use the terms *hokmah* ("wisdom"), *hakam* ("wise"), and *hakam* ("to be wise") to denote both the skill of the artisan (Exod 36:1–7) and the skill of the sage. The texts do not posit the hard, modern distinction between the two, preferring to see them as part of the same phenomenon, what Kneebone rightly calls "expertise." Wisdom in the tradition of Israel is a practice cultivated over time through the guidance of a teacher who has experienced similar training from a teacher, back to time immemorial. (In fact, ancient people usually assumed that the most ancient humans, with divine help, originated all important things and simply passed on the knowledge.)

The question then becomes, how do the biblical texts envision people acquiring and living out the wisdom they seek to inculcate?

Texts and Their Arguments

The practice of wisdom acquisition cannot easily be separated from the content acquired, but it is worth reflecting on the differences by examining how the biblical texts think about learning. If we think of wisdom as expertise in living, as a way of finding voice in the world, then how that happens deserves attention, especially in a world of mass advertising and the commodification of all possible experiences.

The wisdom texts of the Christian Bible do show signs of the fostering of wisdom as a practice. These signs fall into several broad categories,

5. Kneebone, *Expert*, 238.

including the creation of pithy aphorisms, the interrogation of prior ideas ("conventional wisdom"), the formation of intimate communities of learning, and the veneration of the teacher. These texts presuppose a close connection between the making of texts and the making of lives. Consider each element in turn.

From observation to aphorism. Proverbs 24:23 introduces a new section of the book with the rubric, "these also belong to the sages," indicating the plural origins of the sayings in the book, or perhaps better, a tradition of creating, preserving, transmitting, and reflecting upon short sayings. These sayings represent the considered opinion of their collectors. That is, they were selected from among other options by a series of collectors in view of their overall understanding of the nature of a prudential life.[6] Most of the aphorisms in Proverbs and Ecclesiastes are not overtly theological—they rarely speak of God, temple, priests, sacrifices, or even prayers, and they have little role in Jewish or Christian liturgy or theological reflection at any period of those communities' histories. Yet they do appear in the biblical canon.

The prologue of Proverbs (1:2–6) sets out to instill three kinds of virtues: intellectual virtues ("knowing wise instruction"); social and ethical virtues ("righteousness, justice, and equity"); and practical virtues ("cunning, shrewdness"). Most of all the book wishes the person to "honor God" by living prudently. That prologue is itself the result of extreme compression of thought as the entirety of human life is distilled into a few basic orientations. The wisdom it celebrates and tries to inculcate has multiple, mutually reinforcing layers. This wisdom takes the form of character formation, healthy close relationships, just social relationships, the disciplining of language, and proper use of resources, among other topics.

Their cultivation of the art of epitomizing wisdom in very brief form, the proverb, says something about the ancient sages' conception of the aspectual nature of truth and its usefulness in ordinary life. For instance, a saying may caution against gossiping about one person while disputing with another because the verbal gaming will backfire, rather than because of an abstract theory of good and evil language (Prov 25:9–10). Or a string of proverbs can explore the relationship between a ruler and his (usually "his" in the ancient world) counselors:

6. See the discussion in Michael V. Fox, *Proverbs 1–9*, Anchor Bible 18A (New York: Doubleday, 2000), 9–11.

> Elohim's glory is to hide a matter,
>> and kings' glory is discerning a matter.
> Heaven is above and earth below—
>> but there is no discerning the heart of kings.
> Remove the dross from silver,
>> and the smith can produce an object.
> Remove the evil from the king's presence,
>> and his throne will stand on justice. (Prov 25:2–5)

The first line contrasts the divine sovereign with the human one, but the contrast bespeaks their symbiotic relationship, a sort of sagacity game that rulers and their courts play with God. The second line sets forth one of those secrets, the inscrutability (therefore, unpredictability) of both divine and human kings at least where their subjects are concerned. And the last two lines propose a way forward in which kings will pursue righteousness as a silversmith pursues a good vessel. The just kingdom becomes a work of art just as much as a silver bowl or bracelet.

Proverbs knows, of course, that kings may be stupid or wicked, and that tyranny and anarchy remain possibilities at every turn. The task must be navigating an uncertain world while finding as much guidance as possible. The only thing that one can control is oneself, and so the taming of the actions and emotions becomes the highest goal.

Interrogation and dialogue. This taming of the human subject and our expectations for life occupies the thinking of Ecclesiastes, and in a different way, Job. By arranging proverbs in ways that trigger further thought (see Eccl 12:9), these books create discussions about the minutiae of life and allow a wider understanding to grow from small resources into larger ones.

One technique of wisdom cultivation comes also from questions that invite dialogue. The old cliché "there's no such thing as a dumb question" is obviously not true. There are many dumb questions, and some people insist on asking them again and again. But sometimes the unexpected or even unwelcome question opens up possibilities for discovery. Some wisdom texts exploit the possibilities of good questions.

For example, the Epistle of James repeatedly asks its readers questions:

If somebody enters your synagogue sporting a gold ring and fancy clothes, and at the same time a poor person comes in wearing rags, and you pay attention to the one wearing fancy clothes and say, "you sit here in the good spot" but say to the poor person, "stand over there or sit near my footstool," aren't you discriminating among yourselves and showing yourselves to be judges with evil views? (Jas 2:2–4)

What's the profit, my brothers and sisters, if somebody claims to have faith but has no works? Can faith save that person? (Jas 2:14)

Can the same spring emit soft and hard water? My brothers and sisters, can a fig tree bear olives, or a grapevine figs? (Jas 3:11–12)

What is your life? (Jas 4:14)

In each case, the well-timed question forces the reader to consider assumptions about reality (fig trees do not bear olives; favoritism occurs often in a status-conscious society). Part of that reality must be the nature of God and the commitment of the follower of Christ to imitate God insofar as possible. Since God shows no favoritism to rich or poor but opens the storehouses of grace to all on an equal basis, a community worshiping God cannot justify accepting the hierarchies and power politics of the cultures of which they are part. In James, as in other wisdom texts and good teaching more generally, the question, used strategically, enlivens the flow of assertions and proofs to invite the reader to consider the merits of the wisdom text's case. In answering that invitation, the ideal reader must try to grow wiser.

Intimate communities. When we speak of the "ideal reader," we must mean the sort of reader these texts seek to create. Obviously, individuals may misunderstand or disbelieve what they read or try to domesticate it while pretending to accept it. Yet the biblical wisdom texts presuppose different sorts of readers, more serious, more critical, more self-aware.

The biblical wisdom texts frequently name their readers, though in different ways. Proverbs speaks of the "son," the young person, probably originally an elite male, who will learn the ideas, values, and affections of the "father," the teacher of wisdom. Yet the gendered nature of the sayings is not usually difficult to work around. Similarly, the epilogue to Ecclesiastes in a sort of "dear reader" statement describes the collection's author as one who curated words that could be either nails or goads, both sharp objects that either provide stability or prod to action (Eccl 12:11). For that work, the actions of the wise as they pass on the collected insights of their community all point toward honoring the creator, YHWH. In yet another case, Job occasionally winks at the reader, breaking the fourth wall, as in Job's humorous wish that his words should be written in a book or inscribed on stone as a monument (Job 19:23–24).

But the most obvious nods toward communities of readers occur in later texts like Wisdom of Solomon or Ecclesiasticus (Sirach). Written in the late first century BCE, Wisdom of Solomon explicitly addresses kings and rulers (Wis 1:1; 6:1), but this element is clearly fictive. The real audience is those readers who can shift with the text between prayer to God and observations about wisdom and folly, which the book equates to ethical and unethical living, respectively. The book celebrates the superiority of Torah and Jewish wisdom to pagan thought. A pious community of people is in view in this book that is a "handbook on paideia."[7]

Similarly, the prologue to the Greek translation of Ecclesiasticus (Sirach) describes the book's task as the inculcation of *paideia* and *sophia*. The book's translator was the grandson of its author, who had written in Hebrew. The work had moved from the land of Israel to Alexandria, where it gained some currency among Greek-speaking Jews. The translator's prologue was also the book's first commentary (as far as we know), and it describes the book's literary background as a companion of "the law, prophets, and other ancestral books" (Prologue 1). Those learned in the Scriptures might also profit from this new work, or as the prologue says, "those who love learning and are familiar with these things might make rather more progress in living according to the law" (Prologue 13–14). That is, the grandson saw his grandfather's book as a companion to wise, faithful Jews. The community would

7. Jason M. Zurawski, "Paideia: A Multifarious and Unifying Concept in the Wisdom of Solomon," in *Pedagogy in Ancient Judaism and Early Christianity*, ed. Karina Martin Hogan, Matthew Goff, and Emma Wasserman (Atlanta: Society of Biblical Literature, 2017), 195–214.

follow the guidance of Joshua son of Eleazar son of Sirach in pursuing wisdom, honoring the priesthood and the memory of the ancients, all themes in the book.

The New Testament wisdom texts are even more explicit in their identification of the community of readers. They are coextensive with those who follow the long tradition of wisdom especially as Jesus explicated it (see the discussion of the Sermon on the Mount below). James speaks of "the twelve tribes in diaspora" (Jas 1:1), explicitly connecting its message to the history and ongoing life of the Jewish communities around the Roman Empire. First John addresses its readers as "children," in the manner of Proverbs (1 John 5:21). And the Sermon on the Mount and the Sermon on the Plain speak of their hearers as those following Jesus. Audience-building is a complicated matter for all texts, but these do call upon the readers to think about and try to actualize the ideas being stated.

The veneration of the teacher. Along with attention to the form and content of wisdom and the character of the student, these texts frequently speak of the teacher. The Sermon on the Mount cautions against "false prophets," teachers who enter the community and do exorcisms but fail to follow Jesus's teachings (Matt 7:15–23), and the literary framework around the sermon contrasts Jesus's teaching with that of other Torah teachers, also wise men, who nevertheless lack the authority of the soon-to-be-risen Lord (Matt 7:29; cf. 28:18).

The Jesus tradition, however, marks a special development of Israel's wisdom in that definitive wisdom stems from one person, the sage above all sages, Jesus. That extreme ranking of wise persons does not exist elsewhere in the biblical wisdom texts, nor could it, given the Christian understanding of Jesus's person and role. In the older texts, and to some extent in a work like James, there can be many teachers as long as they also pursue wisdom in their words and lives. (And even the Gospel of Matthew steps back toward that broader view when Jesus in Matt 28:19–20 transmits his authority to the apostles as transmitters of his teaching.) These teachers have learned from their teachers, reflecting on the ancient words and applying them to new situations, as we will explore below in the discussion of Job, and as the already cited conclusion of Sirach also shows. The teacher remains an important figure, not because he or she knows all, but because the art of teaching merely extends the art of learning to another level.

In his study of wisdom education as a model for current communities of faith, Charles Melchert speaks of teaching through indirect communication leading to a response of awe and ongoing reflection. In that sort of approach, "learners repeatedly 'get it wrong'" and "the master-teacher expects this of apprentices and finds ways to make the mistakes occasions for more learning."[8] That insight is an important one for understanding the biblical wisdom texts and their use in the church. Far from hectoring students into a life of blind obedience or conformity, these texts try to make students over time into teachers.

This view, if correct, as we believe it is, should prompt a rethinking of the overall social location of wisdom. In modern scholarship, texts like Proverbs, Job, and Ecclesiastes often wear the label "conservative" or "elitist," labels usually sporting a pejorative edge. These works reflect high levels of education and influence, though not the topmost levels of society for the most part. They do reflect the views of some members of elites. But what of that? In our contemporary context, the distrust of expertise and experts has come to support the creation, mostly by the political and religious Right, of a post-truth society. Maybe a little more respect for expertise would be good for us.

Summary. That reclamation of "elite" thinking would take us much further afield than we wish to go now, and entails risks of understanding that we do not wish to take on board. It is far more important to think about the biblical texts expositing Israel's wisdom as part of an ecology of meaning-making. The landscape of wisdom brings together teachers and learners around both pressing questions and curated observations. These texts cultivate a sense of continuity across boundaries of generations and experiences, fostering a way of speaking, thinking, and living that reframes many of the relationships of life in view of deeper concerns.

A couple of cases usefully illustrate these dynamics of the biblical wisdom texts.

---

8. Charles F. Melchert, *Wise Teaching: Biblical Wisdom and Educational Ministry* (Harrisburg, PA: Trinity Press International, 1998), 285.

The Book of Job

Some of the themes of wisdom appear in the first test case we will consider, the book of Job. The book has excited interpreters since at least the second century BCE in texts like the Testament of Job and the Qumran Targum of Job, as well as in the Septuagint's abbreviated version of the book.[9] With its many voices articulating competing points of view,[10] the book models a vigorous conversation centering around the questions of whether God rules the universe well, how wise people should live in response to suffering, and how we might know anything about the divine movements in the world, among other questions. It would be difficult to do justice to the whole book of Job at this point, so we will make only a few observations that bear on its conception of the role of wisdom teacher.

In his first riposte to Job, responding to the harrowing lament of chapter 3, Eliphaz asks,

If someone tested a word with you, would you be weary?
But who could hold in the words?
You instructed many,
and you strengthened drooping hands.
Your words helped up those who had tripped,
and you braced buckling knees. (4:2–4)

Eliphaz expresses frustration at Job's lack of self-control and, indeed, extreme language embracing death rather than life. He contrasts Job's prior role as a teacher, a role Job himself celebrates in chapters 29–31, with his current behavior. For Eliphaz, and presumably the readers of the book and even the character Job himself, the teacher of wisdom

9. A good study of medieval Jewish responses to the book and important modern correspondences to them appears in Robert Eisen, *The Book of Job in Medieval Jewish Philosophy* (Oxford: Oxford University Press, 2004).

10. On the dialogical nature of the book, see Carol Newsom, *The Book of Job: A Contest of Moral Imaginations* (Oxford: Oxford University Press, 2009). On the book as parody and attempts to tame or undercut the parody, see Bruce Zuckerman, *Job the Silent: A Study in Historical Counterpoint* (Oxford: Oxford University Press, 1991). See also Mark W. Hamilton, *A Theological Introduction to the Old Testament* (New York: Oxford University Press, 2018), 211–21.

should use words to support vulnerable people by forming their character ("instruct," from the Hebrew *yasar*, which always has a disciplinary dimension). As modern life coaches know, helping someone grow through failure does not mean sugarcoating the failure but equipping the pupil to learn from mistakes and do better next time. Eliphaz thinks that Job carried out that role well in the past, but that his lament goes much too far in wishing for death and not turning to the divine realm for counsel or even consolation.

Eliphaz's introduction, like much else in the book of Job, cuts in several directions. Perhaps he is right that a teacher should be firm yet gracious when guiding a person in distress. Does Eliphaz live up to that ideal? Job's answer in chapters 6–7 would indicate that Job did not believe that Eliphaz's intervention met that standard. Job replies to the increasingly critical speech of his friend with a series of rhetorical questions:

> Teach me and I will shut up,
>> and help me understand where I went wrong.
> How forceful are straightforward words,
>> but what does a rebuke from you rebuke?
> Can you tally up the rebuke of words
>> as though the words of the afflicted were mere wind? (6:24–26)

Job questions the tone of Eliphaz's teaching. Responding to lament with rebuke cannot be appropriate because that rhetorical move does not address the realities behind the lament. Yet not replying to blasphemy must also be inappropriate. The teacher, then, faces a dilemma in assessing both the surface meanings of the words and the emotions driving them when the two layers do not nicely coincide. Job thinks Eliphaz has seen only the surface of the words, not the emotional, affective life of the person speaking them, much less the actions of God that prompted them in the first place. Eliphaz's and Job's first exchange, and in truth the book as a whole, then, presents the reader with the prospect of two teachers dueling over the meaning of their role and the content of wisdom. The wisdom teacher must acquire a finely tuned ear for the nuances of human suffering in order to formulate a proper response.

Later in the book, the Elihu speeches explore the limits of human understanding of divine speech and the possibility of learning from our griefs, or what Rüdiger Lux has called a "pedagogy of suffering."[11] Suffering has a "communicative and pedagogical" (*kommunicative und pädagogische*) function under certain circumstances, which the wise sufferer and her wise teacher (*Seelsorger*, or "pastor") must discern. How one discerns the meaning of suffering, among other experiences, must be an ongoing work of the community studying a book like Job or engaging the sort of suffering it investigates.

Part of that discernment, as well as the questioning of its possibility, comes in the final section of the book, chapters 38–42. Here at last and contrary to all expectations, YHWH speaks, answering Job from the whirlwind, both instructing him and waiting for his response. These chapters have been read in several ways, with differences deriving chiefly from the competing appraisals of the extent of the irony in the words of YHWH, Job, and the narrator. Perhaps the multiple possibilities of interpretation were deliberately provoked by the book's author, who may have wished to end the book just as ambiguously as it began. Or perhaps it would be possible to come to at least a few points of agreement.

The question is, what do the divine speeches and Job's responses to them mean? YHWH's opening salvo is often taken as a way of telling Job to shut up and stop poking his nose where it does not belong. Given the book's overall interest in teaching and learning, that reading seems problematic. In the first divine speech, YHWH invites Job to consider the very structure of the universe as a temple in which the "sons of God sing for joy" (38:7), the sea knows its limits, and the multifarious forces of nature operate in majestic unconcern for humanity's opinions about them, while also creating space for human flourishing. Job must consider the theater of the cosmos, recognizing his own limited role, the fragility of his understanding, and the inadequacy of his language. He responds to this opening speech of YHWH's, with its repeated queries "do you know?" and "who?" and "how?", by answering, "I am insignificant. How can I respond to you? I put my hand over my mouth" (40:4). That gesture of deference mirrors precisely the courtly behavior visible in Persian reliefs depicting subordinates of the king, and closer to home, Job's own description of his former (elite) subjects deferring

---

11. Rüdiger Lux, *Hiob im Räderwerk des Bösen*, Biblische Gestalten 25 (Leipzig: Evangelische Verlagsanstalt, 2012), 218.

to his greater wisdom (29:9). Far from being an ironic statement or a snarl at an overpowering and irresistible deity, Job's response shows the proper attitude of the student in over his head.

At the end of the book, YHWH rectifies Job's situation as well as possible, compensating him with punitive damages for his trouble. The provocateur *has-satan,* who helped trigger the perfect storm overwhelming Job (and vicariously, the reader), vanishes entirely, and the friends shift for a defense before a deity irritated by their abandonment of their friend. The book's ending raises questions about the role of the sage again, underscoring Eliphaz's original and correct insight that the wise person should comfort the sufferer, allowing that person to lament properly and offering solidarity and empathy rather than pat answers. YHWH does not comfort Job, but also does not crush him or leave the friends' assault on him unanswered.

Teaching a book that reflects intensely on wisdom's elusiveness, mystery, and power for positive change challenges both student and teacher at several levels. Simply following the poetry's imagery and arguments is already a difficult task. In part, we must repeatedly make decisions about tone of voice: how ironic or how straightforward is a given statement? If an image can have more than one significance, which do we follow, or do we follow more than one path? All of that is challenging enough.

But the larger challenge of Job comes from its rigorous honesty about the mysterious nature of wisdom. The wise person knows the limits of his or her insights. The godly person knows the barriers to comprehending the ways of God. Wisdom inevitably leads to awe, a profound fascination with the terrifying beauty of the world and the still more terrifying beauty of God.

The Sermon on the Mount

Like Job, the Sermon on the Mount (our second test case) is undoubtedly one of the most commented upon texts in all the Christian Bible, for obvious reasons. It presents in short compass the core ethical teachings of Jesus and the early church, challenging Jesus's followers to live free from violence or its causes. The radical vision of human existence characteristic of the sermon has inspired many people over the centuries, both Christians and others.

The text itself both begins and ends with direct references to the pursuit of wisdom in terms characteristic of Israel's Bible. The opening places Jesus as a teacher on a mountain, analogous to Moses at Sinai, and the end describes possible responses to the sermon in terms of the Two Ways, a well-known device for understanding moral decision-making, which appears in the Didache and other texts from the turn of the era. The sermon concludes,

> Everybody who hears these words of mine and does them I will compare to a wise man who built his house on the bedrock. When the rain fell and rivers flooded and the winds blew on that house, it didn't fall because it was built on bedrock. And everybody who hears these words of mine and does not do them, I will compare to a stupid man, who built his house on the sand. When the rain fell, the rivers flooded, and the winds blew on that house, it fell. Its fall was dramatic. (Matt 7:24–27)

In other words, the words of the sage Jesus invite humans to learn how to live, to act consistently in a particular direction. Those following Jesus, the Gospel of Matthew asserts, will brave the storms of life well.

Before the Protestant Reformation, most interpreters of the Sermon on the Mount assumed that it laid out a set of behaviors to be lived, a way of imitating Jesus himself.[12] As Thomas Aquinas put it, "a person should build just as Christ did" (*quod hoc debet aedificare sicut Christus*).[13] He goes on to insist that hearing does no good without action, citing also James 1:23, and that intellectual understanding without commitment and attention to the affections will prove unable to withstand temptation.[14] That perspective reflects a widespread view in the patristic and medieval understanding of the text, and it is our understanding as well.

This reading changed with Luther's radical critique of both law and the human capacity for good works. Luther accepted the plain sense of the text that the sermon enjoins acts of obedience and piety, but also

---

12. For a brief survey of the history of interpretation, see Ulrich Luz, *Matthew 1–7*, trans. Wilhelm C. Linss (Minneapolis: Fortress, 1989), 218–23.

13. Thomas Aquinas, *Commentary on the Gospel of Matthew, Chapters 1–12*, ed. Aquinas Institute; trans. Jeremy Holmes and Beth Mortensen (Lander, WY: Aquinas Institute for the Study of Sacred Doctrine, 2013), §674.

14. Aquinas, *Matthew*, §675.

entered into a lengthy discussion about the relationship between grace and merit, pitting the two against each other in ways that seem alien not just to Second Temple Judaism in general but to the Sermon on the Mount in particular. He insists that peoples' works do not merit God's favor or make a person one whit more a Christian since that status comes through baptism and the acceptance of God's mercy. Rather, he insists, the call to good works and the promise of merit have a more localized significance as God's consolation of suffering believers. Although all in Christ are saved, "yet there will be a distinction in the glory with which we shall be adorned." Merit and morality must be relativized.[15] Luther's attack fell chiefly on what he thought of as human-made patterns of good works, including the asceticism characteristic of monastic communities. He drew a sharp contrast between Christ's commands for good works and those "good works" promoted by the church of his time, most of which seemed calculated to distinguish a few elite practitioners from the run-of-the-mill Christian. For Luther, such pursuits of good works and merits simply betrayed a lack of trust in God's mercy and were therefore out of bounds.

The influence of Luther's reading could hardly be overstated, and for many Christians today, the Sermon on the Mount seems an unattainable ideal, and the keeping of its demands just a new form of works righteousness. Yet that reading, also common in popular evangelicalism, seems fundamentally to misunderstand the sermon and, indeed, the relationship between human actions and God's. Instead of Jesus's rigorous demands for the pursuit of a wise life, we have on offer a cheap grace. Paradoxically, reading the sermon as a vision of human life that must always elude us makes it possible for Christians to succumb to the very sins the text calls its readers to leave.

Thanks in part to the social gospel and related theological movements as well as to the pre-Reformation tradition, taking the sermon at face value has become more common in the past century and a half. It seems clear that Matthew understood Jesus to be explicating a set of commitments based on the right ordering of one's affections (as Aquinas would have it). The person who hungered and thirsted for justice, who longed for peace, and all the rest of the attributes blessed in the

---

15. Martin Luther, *The Sermon on the Mount*, trans. Jaroslav Pelikan, Luther's Works 21 (St. Louis: Concordia, 1956), §294.

Beatitudes, would behave in the ways that Matthew's Jesus taught as built on bedrock.

Some of this significance of the sermon as well as its role as a teaching document becomes clearer on closer examination of the text's structure. Not only does the outer frame position it as a wisdom text, but, as Ulrich Luz points out, the Our Father sits at the center of the Sermon.[16] The framework for the prayer, like the rest of the sermon, addresses the disciples or would-be disciples as "you," inviting readers to a heightened self-awareness that helps them name their calling as the one who must listen and either act or refuse to act. "You" may address God as "our Father," finding a place in the community that prays together to Israel's God and trusts that God to bring in the kingdom in spite of the constant risk of hunger, enmity from others, and the risks of sin overcoming the self.

The prayer has close ties to Second Temple Jewish prayers, even if it may go too far for the available evidence to think of it as a response to specific Jewish prayers like the "Eighteen Benedictions."[17] The Our Father entered the liturgical life of the early church and it expressed the community's conviction, deriving from Jesus himself, that God would work in the lives of those imitating Jesus in his simplicity, nonviolence, and poverty.

What has prayer to do with the cultivation of wisdom, and what has wisdom to do with Torah? In the Sermon on the Mount, Matthew cites Jesus as calling his disciples to keep Torah in a way that let their righteousness exceed that of the Pharisees, the primary rivals of Matthew's community. The sermon does not imagine the abolition of Torah or even its replacement by a new Torah. Rather, the interpretations Jesus gives in Matthew 5 especially represent a continuity with the law of Moses, a way of actualizing it in real life. The actualization is radical in many ways, no doubt, and the sermon makes few accommodations to human weakness. It invites Jesus's disciples—those who "build their house on bedrock"—to eschew hatred, abusive language, violence, lust, and a range of character-warping attitudes and behaviors. In doing so, they will join him in "fulfilling" Torah.

16. Luz, *Matthew 1–7*, 211–13.

17. But see the discussion in W. D. Davies, *The Setting of the Sermon on the Mount* (Cambridge: Cambridge University Press, 1966), 307–15.

Again, what has this to do with prayer? Most of the wisdom texts in the Old Testament do not emphasize prayer. The practice plays no role in Proverbs. Ecclesiastes advises people visiting the temple to keep their stay short and not bother God (Eccl 5:1–2) and otherwise has little to say about the practice. Job does consider prayer, often drawing on themes and images familiar from the Psalms, but its hero's torturous interactions with God seem extreme within the context typical of Israelite or biblical piety. So, none of these works connects prayer to moral life in the way the Sermon on the Mount does.

A text that does make such a move is Ecclesiasticus or Sirach. After contemplating the question, "Who will set a guard upon my mouth?" the book of Sirach turns to pray to God: "Lord, father and ruler of my life, do not abandon me to their counsel, suffer me to fall among them" (Sir 22:27–23:6). The prayer goes on to ask God to protect the sage from his own proclivities to abuse language and thought, trying to turn his entire person toward the ethical and spiritual demands of Torah. The prayer tries to shape the affections of the person seeking wisdom so that they will sustain a life of increasing wisdom, and so it appeals to emotions as much as reason.[18]

This linkage among wisdom, Torah, and prayer also informs the Sermon on the Mount. When Jesus's disciples learn to pray for the Kingdom, asking God to become as obedient as the angels, they come to form a community that values certain behaviors and thoughts. The community tests its own affections and commitments, its emotions, so that they can begin to imagine an alternative world and live in ways that help instantiate that world. The framework of the Lord's Prayer (Matt 6:1–6 and 16–18) and the expansion of the prayer in vv. 14–15 all show a strong interest in teaching or what Betz calls "didactic convictions."[19] The wise community defies the common expectations of power and self-promotion. It forms its member through liturgy and instruction about how to live.

18. Núria Calduch-Benages, "Emotions in the Prayer of Sir 22:27–23:6," in *Ancient Jewish Prayers and Emotions: Emotions associated with Jewish prayer in and around the Second Temple period*, ed. Stefan C. Reif and Renate Egger-Wenzel (Berlin: de Gruyter, 2015), 145–59.

19. Hans Dieter Betz, *The Sermon on the Mount*, ed. Adela Yarbro Collins, Hermeneia (Minneapolis: Fortress, 1995), 348.

All of this means two things for understanding the Sermon on the Mount as a wisdom text. First, its audience constitutes a community of learners, the *ekklesia* that Jesus promised to build (Matt 16:18). These learners do much more than memorize texts or authoritative interpretations. They pursue a new world of peace and restraint and justice. They wrestle with the meaning of Torah as a storehouse of divine wisdom. This wrestling involves more than internalizing what had previously been an external command ("don't commit adultery" becoming "don't lust"). It involves outward behaviors that reflect a high estimation of the worth of others before God, a worth exceeding in importance one's own undisciplined desires. In short, the sermon calls for discernment, the spiritual practice of cultivating wisdom by reflection on experience. By discerning the presence of God in the world, the wise person comes to see how human lives may improve.

Second, the sermon points beyond itself to something called the "kingdom." Its ideals are, therefore, both attainable and unattainable, both within human grasp and beyond it. The wisdom of the sermon is a mystery, a new country for exploration rather than a familiar land.

On Wisdom and Its Cultivation

That mystery oozes into the consciousness of wise people and those aspiring to be wise through a long process of learning in a community committed to wisdom. Obviously, it is possible to acquire a sort of wisdom in a society gone mad, the sort of wisdom survivors of the concentration camps might attain. But as Nadezhda Mandelstam says of the Stalinist purges and the Gulag, "the elimination of witnesses was, indeed, part of the whole program."[20] One need not experience the sort of hell Stalin or Hitler created to see that erasing wisdom can be a goal of some systems, and that survival in such a world entails the acquisition of a sort of wisdom.

But by and large, we do not live either in heaven or hell, and the wisdom we acquire is of a happier sort, even if it does rest often on the pedagogy of suffering, as Job teaches its readers. That is because another pedagogy is also in play, a pedagogy of emotions aimed at

20. Nadezhda Mandelstam, *Hope Against Hope: A Memoir*, trans. Max Hayward (New York: Atheneum, 1970), 88.

proper pleasure. Wise teachers, wise learners, and wise communities do much more than transmit information. They interrogate the emotional lives of people and nudge them in particular directions. This pedagogy shines through in the Sermon on the Mount, which pushes its audience to redirect its affections toward God and the neighbor, to keep in check the worst affections of the human heart. This sort of pedagogy does not crush feelings or censor them in unhealthy ways, but it also does not accept the cliché that all feelings are equally valid or that we should be spontaneous at all times. Many desires of the heart will, if acted upon, lead us to the sort of hell we most earnestly wish to escape.

The consequences of the failure to direct the emotions toward good ends appear all over western society today. On the religio-political Right, the brazen celebration of political autocracy, the denigration of sexual or racial minorities, and the denial of even the bare facts of climate change, much less the notion of climate justice, all point toward a deep spiritual disease that unfortunately has also found a thriving incubator in parts of the church in the United States and elsewhere. On the secular Left, the anarchy of values that prevailed after the thorough discrediting of communism as a path to a glorious future is giving way, haltingly, to a search for greater sanity. Whether that sanity will arrive in time to stop the worst excesses of the Right is anybody's guess.

This sort of assessment is obviously loaded in many ways and will arouse controversy. That sort of troublemaking does not interest us much. The larger question is how the church can cultivate the emotional life necessary to the pursuit of wisdom and how the Bible could help us do so.

In her discussion of the proper role of the emotions in a sustainable pluralistic, liberal society, Martha Nussbaum argues that a healthy liberal society must celebrate its own commitment to justice and freedom, including its commitment not to commit to a single theory of the ultimate good of humankind.[21] That discussion deserves serious attention from theologians and pastors in part because the illiberalism against which she inveighs sometimes hijacks Christian language and symbols while distorting the core values of the faith. Many Christians are seduced precisely by the illiberalism she decries.

21. Martha Nussbaum, *Political Emotions: Why Love Matters for Justice* (Cambridge: Belknap/Harvard University Press, 2013).

However, the church espouses a view of the ultimate good of humankind, even though part of loving our neighbors as ourselves must be engaging different ideas with respect and creativity. The cultivation of the emotions and affections, the choice about what we value and therefore do, undergirds the wisdom traditions of the Bible and their use in the church.

The texts speak, for example, of delight as a proper stance for the seeker of wisdom. This pleasure can be in the sage's accumulation of delightful words (Eccl 12:10), or even in the pleasure of arguing with God (Job 9:3, though used ironically, no doubt). The language of pleasure may apply to keeping Torah and finding the consequences of doing so in just and verdant relationships (Ps 19:7–14[8–15]). The peace of mind that accompanies freedom from worrying about display or even survival brings pleasure (Matt 6:25–34). Far from eschewing pleasure, the wisdom texts of Israel and the church find pleasure in an ordered life pursuing deeper understanding and richer relationships with others.

These two pedagogies, one of sorrow and one of pleasure, mutually reinforce each other in the wisdom texts of the Bible and may do so in the church's ongoing life. Neither can lead to wisdom without the other, and neither can cancel out the other. Every pastor knows this from experience, and every church member suspects it even when the language to describe the intertwining of the two realities of life seems lacking. In our next chapter, we take up the question of how to actualize both.

CHAPTER 7

Challenges and Invitations

To this point, we have explored four modalities of the Bible as it works in communities of faith. The texts that the church received from, and shares with, the Jewish people as well as the additional texts stemming from the apostles and their immediate successors all point toward communities that tell stories to understand themselves, vivify the stories in ritual, practice self-examination and self-critique, and cultivate the arts of a wise life. The church does those things imperfectly, but it does them. The healthy interaction of these elements in the church's life with Scripture creates the possibility of inhabiting a world free from obsessive consumerism or political violence. A worshiping, creative, self-reflective people of the story can experience a new freedom and a new responsibility. They can become people of peace.

Settling into such a landscape requires, in part, the reclamation of the Bible. We do not try to go "back to the Bible" but forward to it. We do not think that the Bible provides a blueprint for all possible aspects of contemporary life. It is not a constitution or book of discipline for church organization, but something far more important. The church has always found in its canon the resources for spiritual and moral renewal, for a growing awareness of the work of God, and so for a richer life for human beings. Moving forward toward it bespeaks the text's ability to point beyond itself to the realm of the divine.

Now, however, we must face a question. How can we teach Scripture in contemporary contexts so that the church can become more fully a harbinger of the realm of peace and justice that Jesus calls the kingdom of God? We address the question here in five steps. First, we sketch the contemporary contexts in which the Bible functions. Second, we zoom in on the Bible in these contexts and consider the opportunities and challenges of a context-oriented theological approach to the use of the Bible. Third, we define some of the aims of Christian teaching.

Fourth, we move from the challenges of the moment to solutions in transformational teaching and learning. And fifth, we offer invitations we believe Scripture in our intertwined contexts offers. The movement from imperfectly understood problem to partial solution reflects both the need to act in an uncertain environment and the hopefulness with which we must do so.

Challenges and Opportunities of a Context-Oriented Approach

To begin with context: mapping the contemporary setting of the church in the United States and the Global North poses all sorts of problems. In a world of eight billion people inhabiting hundreds of different, though interlocking, cultures, how can we possibly speak meaningfully of contemporary contexts, or even a single one? Almost any generalization can trigger objections from someone noting an exception. We always need to consider intertwining social contexts (class, gender, race, family structures) as well as physical geography and other features of human life.

At the same time, some factors do seem to operate across many boundaries. These include

- The ubiquity of technology facilitating instantaneous communication. When we give an exam in our classroom, for example, we have to ask students to close their laptops, put away their phones, and remove their smart watches just to ensure that the work they do will be their own.
- An erosion of the local and particular, the surrender of long histories and indigenous art forms to a highly commercialized media culture, as well as many forms of resistance to that erosion.
- A profound discontent with old forms of social organization and the creation of new ones of uncertain duration or significance exhibited by the church in the United States and most of the Global North.
- An epochal shift in the centers of Christianity from the Global North to the Global South. The church of the Global North has just begun to think through what that shift means for its theology, power structures, and discharge of obligations to others. The most important commonality of our time is its lack

of commonality. After three years of wrestling with a global pandemic and its aftermath, pastors and other church leaders recognize the impossibility of returning to the past, but we have not yet understood the new normal.

In such an age of uncertainty, many people, especially young people, have become dissatisfied with the world that their elders have created for them. The commodification of experience in which their very lives are the thing bought and sold in the virtual marketplace, produces a great disquiet into which the church must find ways to enter if it is to bear witness to the redeeming work of God. The spiritual vacuum created by consumerism is increasingly filled with a narrow nationalism and extreme anti-intellectual forms of religion, or else by a kind of self-indulgent life of boredom. What will do on awakening from the American Dream? The critique of religion in general, and of Christianity in particular, comes at times from those seeking to be spiritual but not religious, which can mean a protest against the church's seeming abandonment of its core concerns with worship and moral formation.

For the Bible in particular, the news is mixed. While the Sunday school movement had as its three basic commitments, conversion, studying the Bible, and teaching the Bible, many of the ecclesiastical practices that flourished over the past two hundred and forty years, thanks to that movement, have fallen on hard times. The cognitive and affective dimensions of church educational programs followed public schooling models and became increasingly less formative or transformative than merely informative.

Many churches experience one or more of the following problems:

- a disinterest among adults in religious education of any sort, leading to declining participation in opportunities for learning and growth
- the failure to interest or involve teenagers after the eighth grade
- a sharp and lasting disconnection between the moral and spiritual concerns of church members (much less outsiders) and the church's formational curricula
- inattention to the reality of religious pluralism and its potential for deepening learning

- neglect of the costs and benefits of globalization
- declining biblical and theological literacy

Some attempts have been made to quantify these trends, as in the American Bible Society's studies that we reported earlier. The downward spiral of Bible reading signals a deeper reality, the decline of Christendom in the Global North, and in the United States in particular. The past few years have also made clear the failure of many parts of the church to foster a moral culture consistent with the mercy and love of neighbor called for in Scripture. Charges of antisemitism, misogyny, racism, and homophobia lodged against the church by the critics of US Christianity, including many who wish to remain Christian, even if sometimes unfair, seem more credible than any of us should find comfortable. Our past teaching ministries have often failed to present our mission in winsome ways. Finding a way forward in a context partly of our own creation challenges the church to return to its core values and practices.

The recent COVID-19 pandemic has exposed cracks in the edifice of the church in the United States and elsewhere, apparently accelerating the process of unchurching that had begun years earlier (since the peak of church membership in the 1960s). A large and growing literature aimed at pastors and other church leaders, as well as at laypersons, has emerged to analyze the new reality and propose ways either to paper over the cracks or reconstruct the building entirely. Any comments on the topic must be in the way of an interim report, with tentative conclusions. Still, the pandemic exposed at least two dimensions: some congregations found new opportunities for creativity as they reimagined their ongoing life. They took advantage of new technologies to build community, and they let go of practices no longer fit for purpose. They tried not to waste the crisis. Other congregations, however, became hotbeds of conspiracy theories and alt-Right politics, determined to carry on as though the death of a million of their fellow citizens meant nothing. The absence of the biblical language of lament and the failure to pursue either the pedagogy of suffering or the pedagogy of rightful pleasure left those churches and their members with few Christian resources for navigating the rapids they encountered.

This failure arose because of prior theological constructions that neglected the embodied nature of the spiritual life and the practices (prayer, *lectio divina*, fasting, etc.) that nurture it. When some parts of the church faced the threat to health, they had no resources for responding as Christians and so fell back on the tribal instincts of white suburbia. The cost of that failure will take decades to tally.

Paradoxically, much of the current US church's crisis springs from its past successes, or rather the ways it invested its energies in cultural practices no longer relevant or meaningful. The spread of the Sunday school movement in the nineteenth and twentieth centuries left in place the then culturally acceptable reality of racial segregation while building atop it a structure of age-segregated groups that tried to bank knowledge, sometimes without much attention to the transition from adolescence to adulthood, the life patterns of unmarried adults or of those of all ages with special needs. Too often, younger people find the church unwilling or unable to make space for their probing questions or doubts, in part because assumptions about the nature of the world do not cross generational boundaries. The art of listening has often gone by the board.

For too many churches, similarly, the family structure glorified in 1950s television seemed a default model despite its almost complete absence from the Bible and abnormality in the experiences of a great many people. The church worshiped the God of Ozzie and Harriet more than the God of Abraham, Sarah, and Hagar. That sloppy thinking about the relationship of the gospel to culture all seemed to work for a time, as the large, but now often almost empty, Sunday school wings of older churches testify. It no longer does in most places. Healthy churches must wrestle with the legacy of the past, eschewing both nostalgia and self-hatred, and seek believable and life-giving futures.

Let us be clear, however. While Christian teachers have a responsibility to name the challenges of our setting as clearly and honestly as possible, including the ways in which the church has contributed to our problems, our task does not end with lament. We bear a responsibility to identify other possibilities, to celebrate the good work done by others, and to encourage imitation of that work. One way for church leaders to take responsibility is to interrogate our own lives and the lives around us through the lens of the four modalities we discussed in previous chapters. What narratives do we see playing out around us? How do we and our neighbors ritualize our experience? What mechanisms exist for bringing about change through reimagining possibilities? What counts as wisdom and how do we acquire it?

The Bible in Interlocking Contexts

A community asking questions like those must also assess where on its landscape the Bible appears and how it lives there. Clearly, the Bible lives and dies at many locations on the current landscape of Christianity in the United States and in the many connections the churches in this country have with others around the world. It appears in liturgy and sermon regardless of the confessional stance or history of a self-identifying Christian group. It usually appears in systems of education, that is, in small home groups and more traditional lecture rooms. It figures in the many missionary and charitable activities that virtually all congregations exercise. Even when the content of sermons, hymns, or prayers varies, Christians of all stripes recognize those acts and their use of Scripture in the hands of others.

The use of the Bible may go awry in several ways as it serves the distortions of Christian practice. One distortion is *doctrinalism*, the reduction of the faith to a set of ideas to be believed without question. In that distortion of the faith, the credal statement, written or unwritten, becomes divorced from the life of piety or ethical commitments, and any questioning of the most minute aspects of the approved dogma threatens the group that has built its identity upon it.

Another distortion is *pietism*, locating "true religion" or "faithfulness" in the conformity of individuals to specific spiritual practices so that those practices define the full extent of the faith. Clichés like "spending quiet time with Jesus" or "accepting him as your personal savior" mask several assumptions, including the possibility that ordinary people may, through dedicated effort, gain direct and continuous access to God more or less unmediated by history, the life of the whole church over time, or the limitations posed by inadequate knowledge or bodily frailty.

Another distortion takes the form of *moralism*, the conviction that one may merit grace by being good boys and girls, often within a fairly limited realm of moral issues. The Bible, in this view, becomes a rule book about sexuality and perhaps a few other discrete topics. And a fourth distortion takes the form of *culturalism*, a conviction that the Bible remains in the past, and the impulses of today must guide behavior.

All of these "-isms" stem from inattention to the multiple layers of meaning that a community of reflective practice may attach to the Bible and its other theological resources. Inadequate attention to the Bible, to the context of the reader, or to the act of reading (or all three) leads to such distortions. Conversely, however, attention to interlocking the contexts in which each of us lives is part of the prime directive of practical theology, including the arts of teaching and preaching Scripture.

In his now classic study of practical theology in North America (mostly anglophone United States plus Canada), Douglas John Hall calls for a contextual theology but cautions against certain dangers of leaning too heavily on context. As he argues, "The danger implicit in any theology which takes seriously the contextual dimension is that it will give way to relativism, and may become too narrowly focused upon its own immediate context."[1] That relativism may be historical or local or something else. It arises whenever concern for the context of the theology overwhelms concern for the tradition the theologian has received as a gift from the past. Hall calls for a "dialogue with our tradition,"[2] that is, an intellectual and spiritual reckoning with all of the texts and practices inherited by the church as a whole and in its several parts. That dialogue may take different forms, but it must happen if the theological work is to have any chance of being truly Christian.

Such a critical dialogue would preserve the church from the various kinds of fundamentalism (including scientific fundamentalism) distorting the tradition as a whole in the interest of accentuating some part of it. It would also help us to move beyond facile moralizing about the biblical text, which notoriously refuses to squeeze into neat categories of commendable and problematic human behavior. For the Bible to continue to be the book with which the church wrestles, the church must attend to its own movements as a wrestler.

That wrestling takes the form of careful reading, intense and uncensored discussion, and a move to application. Yet important aspects of contemporary culture in the United States present obstacles to careful reading. For example, our immersion in media and the technology on which we consume it has made many readers of the Bible what John

---

1. Douglas John Hall, *Thinking the Faith: Christian Theology in a North American Context* (Minneapolis: Fortress, 1989), 111.

2. Hall, *Thinking the Faith*, 117.

Dyer calls the "people of the screen."[3] In his groundbreaking study of the development of Bible study software since the 1980s, primarily by evangelicals but crossing many theological boundaries, Dyer notes studies that show lessening comprehension by those reading texts on screens. The use of hypertexts can render deep reading more difficult and can promote confusion between real understanding and mere accumulation of factoids. The medium is not neutral, but its value depends on the practices of reading that accompany it. Just as the wider distribution of the Bible after the invention of the printing press facilitated both wider education and more opportunities for cranks and charlatans, so too can the addition of the screen to the printed page as a medium of reading the Bible bring either deeper learning or more entrenched ignorance. The difference will lie partly in the medium, but more in the practices that readers adopt to manage the medium. Wisdom is required.

Defining the Means of Teaching the Bible

Our approach to teaching Scripture starts from several orientations. One is the realization that the church has always understood Jesus as a teacher who sought to change the lives of his disciples. Christian religious education is a critical means of maintaining the life of the church and moving it forward in light of Jesus's ministry and commands.

Another is an understanding of Christian religious education as a deliberate, carefully planned, and sustained work cooperating with God to inculcate appropriate knowledge, values, attitudes, life skills, sensitivities, and behaviors consistent with the Christian faith. In other words, such an education concerns the formation of character. The processes of teaching and learning in the church, especially learning of the Bible, ought to help individuals and the community as a whole follow Jesus Christ and live in ways normed by the Christian faith.

Another orientation concerns the aims of teaching. The Bible and other theological resources help the community know and love God, live out God's wisdom, embrace God's love and grace, and grow into persons of faith, hope, and love. The vision of Romans 12:2, transformation through the renewing of the mind in order to do good works,

3. John Dyer, *People of the Screen: How Evangelicals Created the Digital Bible and How It Shapes Their Reading of Scripture* (New York: Oxford University Press, 2023).

provides a valuable touchstone for our thinking. We must help each other interpret experiences in ways that befit a proper understanding of God and neighbor.

In reading the Bible with our full mental apparatus of critical thinking and a sense of wonder and enjoyment, we engage the entire text as a gift to us from Israel and the early church, and so, from God. We place the biblical texts in dialogue with the currents of our own time and use those texts as a critical lens for examining our culture. We reclaim the language of Scripture in liturgy and its images in art and music. And most of all, we embrace its vision of a redeemed humanity.

Yet another basic conviction is that a transformed life cannot occur all at once but requires a lifetime of commitment and effort, as well as trust in the grace and mercy of both God and human beings. The critical approach we bring to bear seeks transformation based on an attitude of trust and hope. Christian faith is lived and loved, celebrated and narrated, critiqued and embraced, all over the course of years.

These ambitious goals demand that the church think of its interaction with Scripture as something that involves all Christians in all their activities as a community. Every activity in the congregation's life implies something about the education of people.

Models of Transformational Teaching and Learning in Context

So far, then, we have the problem and the goal. How do we move toward the goal in light of the challenges we face? Now, we must turn toward possible solutions from the discipline of Christian religious education. Many models of education exist in the marketplace of ideas, and deserve serious consideration. Here we can attend to only a few aspects of education in contemporary contexts. We especially consider the case of the adult learner, since adults remain what Malcolm Knowles called them a half century ago, "a neglected species."[4] Adults remain neglected learners in contexts of Christian religious formation. Yet they have critical roles in the building of the church's present and future. And we focus on the interplay of catechesis and transformational learning as a path toward innovation.

4. Malcolm Knowles, *The Adult Learner: A Neglected Species* (Houston: Gulf, 1973).

At this point, we must acknowledge that several schools of thought compete for influence in the field of Christian religious education. These do not tightly align with confessional commitments, though they do tend to do so. One trend seeks to cure biblical and theological illiteracy by renewed attention to catechesis and apologetics, arguing that the failure to set forth the core ideas and practices of Christianity leads to ignorance of those elements and orphans people from their own faith.[5] This approach takes seriously both expressions of Christian doctrines common to all parts of the church and more localized traditions of denominations and families of denominations. It risks, however, a return to parochialism and when it relies too much on memorization of set answers as in traditional catechisms (a form popularized by Luther and then adopted by both Protestants and Catholics), it can stifle the spiritual imaginations of people and actually undermine learning.

Another approach has been transformational or transformative teaching and learning. Drawing on the work of such thinkers as Paolo Freire and Jack Mezirow, numerous scholars of Christian religious education have proposed paths to human change as a way of understanding the church's work. Working in an environment of massive economic disparities and political repression, Freire saw education as a process of liberation and empowerment—liberation from unjust social structures and empowerment to create new and better ones.[6] Mezirow worked in the United States primarily, but his retrieval of adult education (andragogy) as a legitimate concern has influenced many subdisciplines of education. A summary of his thinking appears in his sentence, "Learning is understood as the process of using a prior interpretation to construe a new or revised interpretation of the meaning of one's experience as a guide to future action."[7] Process-oriented education allows for flexibility and improvisation, and the attention to

---

5. See, for example, D. H. Williams, *Defending and Defining the Faith: An Introduction to Early Christian Apologetic Literature* (New York: Oxford University Press, 2020); Benjamin D. Espinoza and Beverly Johnson-Miller, "Catechesis, Developmental Theory, and a Fresh Vision for Christian Education," *Christian Education Journal* 11 (2014): 8–23.

6. Most famously worked out in Freire's duology, *Pedagogy of the Oppressed* (New York: Seabury, 1970); and *Pedagogy of Hope* (New York: Continuum, 1994).

7. Jack Mezirow and Associates, *Learning as Transformation* (San Francisco: Jossey-Bass, 2000), 5. See also his work *Transformative Dimensions of Adult Learning* (San Francisco: Jossey-Bass, 1991).

meaning-making allows the banking of information to find a proper home as a resource for higher-level thinking rather than an end in itself.

The understanding of religious education, and Christian formation in particular, as a process of transformation has influenced two generations of scholars in the field and, through them, church leaders and their congregations.[8] A rich body of work cutting across confessional lines has emerged.

A good conspectus of that work comes from Edmund O'Sullivan, whose research concentrated on the pursuit of deep wisdom in various forms of spirituality. He wrote,

> Transformative learning involves experiencing a deep, structural shift in the basic premises of thought, feelings, and actions. It is a shift of consciousness that dramatically and irreversibly alters our way of being in the world. Such a shift involves our understanding of ourselves and our self-locations; our relationships with other humans and with the natural world; our understanding of relations of power in interlocking structures of class, race and gender; our body awarenesses [sic], our visions of alternative approaches to living; and our sense of possibilities for social justice and peace and personal joy.[9]

That broad and deep vision of transformational/transformative education encompasses the many interlocking dimensions of human life. For Christians, it captures our need and desire to reclaim the biblical vision of a holistic person being redeemed in their entirety by the creator God.

These two approaches to Christian education often seem at cross-purposes, and some advocates for reclaiming catechesis explicitly critique a transformational approach as leaving too many holes in the

8. E.g., Maria Harris and Gabriel Moran, *Reshaping Religious Education: Conversations on Contemporary Practice* (Louisville: Westminster John Knox, 1998); Thomas H. Groome, *Christian Religious Education* (San Francisco: Harper & Row, 1980); Thomas H. Groome, *Will There Be Faith? A New Vision for Educating and Growing Disciples* (New York: HarperOne, 2011); Debra Dean Murphy, *Teaching That Transforms: Worship as the Heart of Christian Education* (Grand Rapids: Brazos, 2004); Robert Pazmiño, *Foundational Issues in Christian Education: An Introduction in Evangelical Perspective*, 3rd ed. (Grand Rapids: Baker Academic, 2008).

9. Edmund O'Sullivan, "Bringing a Perspective of Transformative Learning to Globalized Consumption," *International Journal of Consumer Studies* 27 (2003): 327 (326–30).

understanding of Christians to be useful.[10] Our own view differs from that perspective. Any educational approach has limits because human persons and communities present too many spiritual, intellectual, aesthetic, and moral complexities to be reduced to formulas, no matter how expansive. True learning inducts the learner into awesome mysteries, hard to contain or define, always just eluding our grasp. In the church, learning occurs through practices that point far beyond themselves, practices like Sabbath-keeping and testimony and the daily carrying out of mundane tasks. A transformational approach is necessary because humans do not learn best by memorizing and regurgitating facts or truth claims.[11]

On the other hand, the recovery of catechesis as a practice deserves serious attention. As professors at a university, many of whose students profess some version of Christian faith, we encounter a majority who have received almost no deep education in Scripture, the history of the church, or core theological ideas. Some from very conservative Bible churches have been indoctrinated into theologies that often distort elements of Christian theology, and students often repudiate that sort of Christianity and the faith more generally, on the assumption that fundamentalism *is* the faith. Excessive certainty plus bad ideas create unbelief. On the other hand, students from more moderate Christian groups often have been taught to equate Christianity with "being nice." Theological ideas get short shrift as being somehow impractical or even obstacles to true piety. These are generalizations, of course, but if the gaps we see in students says anything about the educational work of churches, the verdict cannot be good.

The point is, a comprehensive approach to Christian education in general, including the theologically rich encounter with Scripture, may require a multiprong approach. Beginners, whether children or adults, need basic instruction that looks something like traditional catechesis. But that catechesis need not stifle questioning, especially when the learning is part of a full congregational life of worship, service, and

10. As argued, for example, by Espinoza and Johnson-Miller, "Fresh Vision."
11. On such practices in Christian education, see the essays by several contributors in Dorothy C. Bass, ed., *Practicing Our Faith: A Way of Life for a Searching People*, 2nd ed. (San Francisco: Jossey-Bass, 2010).

fellowship. To the contrary, teachers should encourage learners at all levels to ask "what does this claim mean?" and "how should I live into it?"

What would transformational catechesis look like? Alfredita Tahiri describes a community of learners in a university in Kosovo. Their innovative learning experience, contrary to the long-held assumptions about the nature of university education with its traditions of lecture and memorization, requires several elements: (1) students and professors work together as partners in learning; (2) they remain open to change while (3) agreeing to take responsibility for their own perceptions of reality; (4) they all share life together as members of the learning community; (5) they engage in critical reflection; and (6) they foster the maturity required for dealing with change.[12]

This sort of model has pitfalls, to be sure. Proclamations of equality can mask real disparities of power, and the rhetoric of fellowship may make redress of grievances much more difficult. Celebrating the freedom of the learner can hide that person's own will to power and abusive tendencies. In short, a transformational model of education requires more, not less, attention to the passions and their proper cultivation.

Nevertheless, the challenges facing a transformational approach to education face other types as well. The human capacity for sin does not express itself only in one educational model. Transformational models take seriously the realities of human desires for growth, for greater knowledge and understanding, for effective ways of loving others.

Christian religious educators might formulate the goal of transformation in various ways. The adult learner becomes an imitator of Christ, or grows in the spiritual virtues, or is sanctified, or enters a process of theosis (becoming like God). Those phrases do not all mean quite the same thing, and each has a long history, but the variety on this point should tell us something about the transformation we seek. The church teaches Scripture and engages in other spiritual practices in order to lead a more virtuous and creative life. Transformation, that is, has a telos, a goal. Each of the formulations of that goal says something valuable about it, and collectively they point to its elusiveness. The Christian life participates in a mystery, the divine life with the creation.

---

12. Alfredita Tahiri, "Fostering Transformative Learning: The Role of Professors and Students at the University of Prishtina," *Interchange* 41 (2010): 149–59.

It follows, then, that life with the Bible must allow space for the vitality of searching, questioning, probing, and disagreeing. Practices that enforce conformity undermine themselves, leading either to a disempowered community or to indifference or to repudiation of the entire group's way of life. It also follows that the search for the single right answer must give way to a concern for the process of learning itself and the outcome that is a curious, committed, yet always learning human being.

In her discussion of a way of reading the Bible that surfaces its agrarian elements and their potential meaning for today, Ellen Davis contrasts her way of reading the Bible for constructing a sustainable ethic with other options. The most influential attempts to use the Bible for ethics insist on starting with exegesis, almost as though it were an objective pursuit unsullied by the particularities of human life. She rightly insists, however, that "it is not always possible to do good exegesis as a first step. Sometimes important aspects of a text are not visible to an interpreter—or a whole generation of interpreters—until there has been a reordering of our minds and even our lives. . . ."[13] That is, understanding the Bible's implications for life is a complex activity requiring a range of interpretive tools not easily acquired. Becoming a good reader entails more than understanding Greek or Hebrew syntax or the ins and outs of ancient Near Eastern political thought. Reading for transformation demands self-awareness and love of neighbor or the ability to imagine oneself properly in the mental geography the text is helping create.

We are not far here from Thomas Groome's model of Christian religious education as "life to faith to life," an ongoing spiral of experience and reflection, experimentation and correction, all with guidance from a tradition in the understanding of which the learner grows.[14] In this sort of view, the Bible and the classic creeds become part roadmaps for the spiritual world and part songs sung while traveling through it. Psalms and oracles, proverbs and stories all become part of the language of a community seeking the God to which the words point, rather than banners to salute or weapons to wield.

---

13. Ellen F. Davis, *Scripture, Culture, and Agriculture: An Agrarian Reading of the Bible*, foreword by Wendell Berry (Cambridge: Cambridge University Press, 2009), 27.

14. Groome, *Will There Be Faith?*, esp. 261–97.

Transformational teaching takes advantage of the crises of faith that can arise through encountering the Bible as a difficult book that names hard moral dilemmas and sometimes even portrays God in compromising positions. Readers of the Bible bring to it not only a capacity for finding gaps in the text, but also their own experiences of the seeming absence, indifference, or hostility of God during times of hardship. Indeed, the canon of Scripture itself presupposes recurring existential crises in its readers as they seek to enter the mystery of God's election of Israel and through them, the whole world. Paradox and complexity abound, and that is as it should be. In periods of crisis, we do our best learning. The Bible's God wrestles with life's enigmas beside us.

This acceptance of doubt and wonder as normal highlights a central notion of Christian formation, namely, that it is not linear, but more circuitous. The good teacher must, therefore, be prepared to take a trip along with the student, with the stops on the journey not always known at the outset.

The teacher of the Bible, then, has several qualities. She or he

- encourages students to reflect on and share their feelings with others;
- invites holistic awareness of body and mind, of the whole person;
- has well thought-out convictions but creates space for those of others;
- establishes an atmosphere of trust and care;
- builds trust among students;
- mentors students in their discovery of faith, hope, and love;
- helps with critical reflection on the past so as to build a meaning-making self;
- identifies aspects of the Bible both to learn and to unlearn; and
- questions easy assumptions about theology and other aspects of human existence.

These qualities elicit appropriate commitments from students, who take responsibility for their own learning and for their peers' well-being. This approach, especially appropriate for adults, avoids the pitfalls of authoritarian communities while creating genuine, sustained learning.

Study of the Bible in ways that help transformation requires teachers to set up space for critical reflection, rational argument, honest inquiry into the history of ideas and practices, and the life history that led students to ask questions about faith. Students become more empathetic and careful listeners, appreciative of the ideas of others, including the ideas of the biblical text and the religious traditions of which it is part. Students begin to ask what makes a given text tick. They also explore their own biographies, relationships, ideas, and capacities for good or evil.

Finally, transformational teaching and learning with relation to the Bible not only identifies the ways in which Scripture narrates a community's life, it also creates rituals that actualize that narrative, challenge and reimagine that narrative, and provoke the search for wisdom. Our teaching and learning must help us interrogate how those dimensions of life play out for us. What narratives shape our lives, including those hidden stories lying below the surface of cognition? What rituals reinforce or, alternatively, counteract the core rituals of baptism and Eucharist for us? What do we imagine as a world better than the one we inhabit, and how do we decide among the moral proposals competing for our attention and approval? What do we really consider wisdom, and why? The aim of our teaching Scripture must be to allow its visions of a redeemed humanity to enter our consciousness, to accept its view of reality as a lens through which to interrogate our own (as well as vice versa), and to reclaim its language in liturgy, art, and ethical reflection.

By examining teaching and learning through such a wide-angle lens, we can move beyond the dichotomies both reformers and defenders of the status quo pose between doctrine and life, recognizing that key theological ideas have implications for the whole of our lives as individuals and communities.[15] Emotion and cognition become two intertwined parts of a whole. The individual and the community mutually support each other. And Bible and tradition and a free intellectual life enrich one another rather than live at daggers drawn. Transformation leads to holism, a close cousin of what the Hebrew Bible calls *shalom*.

---

15. A point often made, as for example in John A. Berntsen, "Christian Affections and the Catechumenate," in *Theological Perspectives on Christian Formation: A Reader on Theology and Christian Education*, ed. Jeff Astley, Leslie J. Francis, and Colin Crowder (Grand Rapids: Eerdmans, 1996), 229–51.

Invitations

At this point in the discussion, we have begun to sketch a solution to a problem. Yet a problem/solution approach does not fully do justice to our context, which, like all of human life, is one of sorrow and joy, challenge and opportunity. Rather, we should consider the invitations we have received as a legacy from the church's centuries-long encounter with Scripture.

The first invitation is to enter a hopeful story. John Webster argues against attempts to ground hope in a universal human impulse rather than the story of Jesus of Nazareth, who of course was an observant Jew and worshiper of the God of Abraham, Isaac, and Jacob. The long story of redemption is the source and object of hope, not a feeling. That hope acknowledges the horrors of human history and the myriad ways in which evil shoots through every social structure and behavior. "Yet," Webster writes, "not to speak of history as God's ordered economy is to fail to articulate a primary condition of Christian hope, for hope arises from discernment of our place in God's history with us."[16] That hope does not focus entirely on eschatological expectation either. God, according to Scripture and the traditions flowing out of it, does not work only in the "sweet by and by," but also in the past, present, and future of this world.

In other words, transformational teaching builds on the human need for narrative-making to allow learners to heal from their pasts and build their futures. The cultivation of hope through narrative was an important concern for the biblical writers. Texts like Deuteronomy 30 or Jeremiah 30–33 reflect on the realities of forced migration (the so-called Assyrian and Babylonian exiles) and find even within the exigencies of history the possibility of redemption. These texts come from the unfolding Deuteronomic tradition (probably its latest stages) transforming the narrative of Joshua–2 Kings from an explanation of tragedy to a source of hope. This hope becomes more explicit in texts like Ezra-Nehemiah or Isaiah 40–66. Hope does not promise utopia or ignore the struggles of life but pronounces upon them a "nevertheless."

16. John Webster, "Hope," in *The Oxford Handbook of Theological Ethics*, ed. Gilbert Meilaender and William Werpehowski (Oxford: Oxford University Press, 2005), 297.

A Christian community critically engaging the narrative of the Bible and its own narrative cannot pretend that all is well, and it cannot cruelly ignore suffering by claiming that God will make it all right in the afterlife. It can both lament and repent, and the two ways of relating to experience need each other for true transformation to occur.[17] The community that draws strength from genuine engagement with Scripture, rather, acknowledges the suffering of others, joins that suffering, invites God to join it, and seeks its end in this life.

The second invitation is to join in a ritualized life, a regular communal practice of prayer in its many forms (lament, confession, praise, intercession, supplication, requests for wisdom), whether spoken or silent or sung. According to Matthew and Luke (and their sources), Jesus taught his disciples to pray the Our Father, the oldest bit of Christian liturgy not drawn directly from the Hebrew Bible. Jesus's prayer fits nicely within the context of first-century Judaism, yet it has also lived many other lives in communal worship and private devotion. Accompanying the large and growing body of Christian prayer has been the Eucharist, a great source of encouragement and healing to generations of Christians.[18] As the church in the United States and the Global North renews itself, it should find eucharistic renewal an engine of revival. The ritual practice points Christians to the sufferings of its Lord, as well as to his glory. The Lord's Supper foreshadows the heavenly banquet in which all human needs find satisfaction, and all injuries find healing. And so along with comforting the church, the Eucharist challenges the church to get on with its task of making peace and hungering for justice.

The third invitation is to enter the world of the poet and prophet, to dream of a world better than this one. The prophetic voices of the Bible do not scrap the tradition that preceded them. To the contrary, they build intentionally on past words, images, and ideas to critique both

17. See the discussion in Mark J. Boda, "The Priceless Gain of Penitence: From Communal Lament to Penitential Prayer in the 'Exilic' Liturgy of Israel," in *Lamentations in Ancient and Contemporary Cultural Contexts*, ed. Nancy C. Lee and Carleen Mandolfo, Symposium Series 43 (Atlanta: Society of Biblical Literature, 2008), 81–101.

18. Note the discussion in Ann Morrow Heekin, "Christian Story as Ritual Engagement: The American Liturgical Renewal in the Rise of Narrative Theology," *Proceedings of the 2006 Meeting of the Religious Education Association* https://old.religiouseducation .net/member/06_rea_papers/Heekin_%20Ann.pdf (accessed 13 March 2023).

the story their community has lived out and the many counter-stories told by other communities. Isaiah's questioning of Assyrian power or Revelation's rejection of Rome's shows the sort of courage required by the prophetic mode of communal life. Asking "why?" to the claims of dominant cultures provokes a response. Taking the side of the vulnerable requires both courage in the short run and persistence over time, since oppression can damage the very soul of the oppressed and the oppressor. A community that finds the freedom to serve those in need and to incorporate them within their number and so remove their need can truly be the beloved community.

The fourth invitation is to pursue wisdom. Of course, the desire for prudential behavior is not controversial. Book stores abound in works in the self-help category, a dumbed-down version of the wisdom discourses of many cultures over centuries. The biblical wisdom texts make some space for that sort of wisdom. They also, however, raise the possibility of wisdom as a way of life that results from the disciplining of the passions, not their erasure but their channeling in directions that lead to a more harmonious life. The church encountering the Bible hears the invitation to resist self-indulgence or the enticements of the demagogue. Wisdom is a practice, an art to be cultivated in the formation of an ecosystem of learning. To see things as they are yet without succumbing to cynicism or despair—that is wisdom's promise.

On Challenges and Invitations

Problems, contexts, transformation, and invitation. Here we have not proposed detailed programs or structures to replace those now disintegrating around us. The sort of experimentation required today will need many creative minds working in congregations, cell groups, schools, coffee shops, and other social gatherings. We have tried, then, to sketch the sorts of questions and concerns our era of trial and error can profitably address. Those areas of attention coincide, we believe, with the primary zones of human life to which the Bible itself attends, narrative, ritual, prophecy, and wisdom. We must engage both Scripture and our current contexts with a high level of critical thinking, as well as wonder and joy. Only through such engagement can our experiments in human flourishing succeed on Christian terms.

Conclusion

Human flourishing has been a subtext throughout this work. Christian religious education or education must have as its object the betterment of human beings as well as the praise of God. That is, this form of Christian ministry, like all others, should foster love for God and neighbor. Our book sounds a call to follow such an educational program in regard to the teaching of Scripture. To clarify the nature of this call, we should first retrace our steps and then suggest some paths forward.

Where We Have Been

We have tried to make a straightforward case: the church is the sort of community that narrates its own past. The narrative's plot takes that past from the remotest human ancestors to the people of Israel, whom God called to a life of dignity and discipline. This people, liberated from the thralldom of evil, received guidance in a way of life promoting love of neighbor and justice for all. While it did not always live up to that calling, it received divine mercy and so pioneered a just and peaceful life for the rest of the human race. A Jewish man, Jesus of Nazareth, lived and died as a faithful heir of Israel, and his followers proclaim his death and resurrection as the entry point into the world of God, a world Jesus named the kingdom. Their narrative continues until the present and culminates in the eschaton, when all things will be made new and right. This narrative interacts with others, most notably the ongoing story of the Jewish people, to testify to the faithfulness and mercy of the one God.

In instantiating and revivifying this narrative, the church worships God, building space for prayer, the Eucharist, and other rituals that allow its primal story to live. It also critiques itself and, drawing on its traditions and experiences, constantly replenishes the storehouses of its imagination in order to stay on the path of justice and peace. It also pursues wisdom, often by fits and starts, but nevertheless with a constancy of purpose.

These are the ideals. The reality may differ, but human frailty and failure do not lessen the importance of the goal.

If the church does these things, the presence of these modes of life in the Bible, the church's Scripture, should hardly be surprising. We have discussed at length the arts of storytelling, ritualizing, prophesying, and wisdom-building in the Old and New Testaments, and there is no need to repeat all that. The congruence of the church's needs and the Bible's supply is impressive enough.

That congruence can, we have argued, shape how we teach the biblical texts. We need to attend to the multiple overlapping contexts in which we live, as well as the historical settings of the biblical text itself. The gaps and overlaps are themselves interesting, as interpretation often happens in the interstices. Learning flourishes when uncertainty prevails.

The ministry of teaching Scripture, we claim, needs renewal at many levels. We have focused on adult education, since transformational learning applies primarily to those who can actualize a commitment to change. In a post-Christian environment, as parts of the United States are becoming, the focus on adults will bring new life to congregations and the communities they serve. This focus does not imply a neglect of children, however. Quite to the contrary. We invite a wide-ranging discussion on the nature of ministry to and for children. The texts of the Bible are the common property of all within the orbit of the church, and deep engagement with those texts can be a joint enterprise across generational lines. Yet we believe that the church has too often left such engagement to childhood, failing to help adults think critically about the Bible or about their own faith. It is long since passed time that we did better.

Throughout this discussion, moreover, we have also called for close attention to the contexts of learning and teaching. The church gains nothing from either nostalgia or a reckless disregard for the past. It gains nothing either by identifying a particular ethnicity, class, or gender as a default state for its work, or by pretending that such dimensions of life do not matter. Realism tempered by hopefulness should be our watchword. We must cultivate spiritually mature discernment as a way of life, and we can do so by embracing our lives with Scripture and core practices like prayer and service to others.

Where We Need to Go

Accepting these proposals can, we believe, open the door to new possibilities. These possibilities have not yet made themselves visible, and so we hope our work will invite many others to join the conversation as we seek renewal together. This renewal will occur at several levels of the church's organized life. It occurs in congregations as pastors and other leaders reimagine their lives and work as first of all teachers of a way of life. We recognize that pastors are usually very busy people, who confront repeated calls to rethink their entire workload. But we have to believe that the imaginative work that can occur through the teaching of Scripture (which they do every week anyway) can refresh their self-understandings and revive their relationships with others.

This renewal must also occur at the level of denominations and the emerging quasi-denominational networks that grace the landscape of the free church. Most congregations in the United States are too small to do all the work on their own, but when networked with others can amply serve wide communities of learners. By fronting the task of transformational teaching, such larger networks and their constituent congregations may find that some frustrating aspects of their lives simply fall away. Not every ministry needs to survive for the church to flourish. Some, in fact, should die so that the body as a whole can live.

This reimagination should also affect the seminary, where ministers find their vocational footing in the first place. Many seminaries have dropped programs in Christian religious education, in part because it seemed passé in the face of so many other needs. Programs that inducted religious educators into a school model might well die, but a more imaginative approach to the whole task could reinvigorate just such programs and the churches they serve.

Finally, we acknowledge that much of the future remains obscure. Yet we believe that once the church abandons its obsession with cultural success masquerading as "relevance" and embraces its Lord's call to hunger and thirst for justice, to make peace, to restrain excessive ambition, to embrace the needy, and to mourn with the mourning, we may begin to do the most important work human beings can do. We may join the creator in the work of turning the "formless and void" into a space where goodness flourishes and every tear is wiped away. That, surely, will be enough.

Further Reading

Biblical Theology

Bauckham, Richard. *The Bible in the Contemporary World: Hermeneutical Ventures*. Grand Rapids: Eerdmans, 2015.

Davis, Ellen F., and Richard B. Hays, eds. *The Art of Reading Scripture*. Grand Rapids: Eerdmans, 2003.

East, Brad. *The Church's Book: Theology of Scripture in Ecclesial Context*. Grand Rapids: Eerdmans, 2022.

Goldingay, John. *Reading Jesus's Bible: How the New Testament Helps Us Understand the Old Testament*. Grand Rapids: Eerdmans, 2017.

Johnson, Luke Timothy. *Prophetic Jesus, Prophetic Church: The Challenge of Luke-Acts to Contemporary Christians*. Grand Rapids: Eerdmans, 2011.

McCaulley, Esau, *Reading While Black: African Biblical Interpretation as an Exercise in Hope*. Downers Grove, IL: IVP Academic, 2020.

Practical Theology

Andrews, Dale P., and Robert London Smith, eds. *Black Practical Theology*. Waco, TX: Baylor University Press, 2015.

Bass, Diana Butler, and Joseph Stewart-Sicking, eds. *From Nomads to Pilgrims: Stories from Practicing Congregations*. Bethesda, MD: Alban, 2005.

Bass, Dorothy C. *Christian Practical Wisdom: What It Is, Why It Matters*. Grand Rapids: Eerdmans, 2016.

Jennings, Willie James. *The Christian Imagination: Theology and the Origins of Race*. New Haven: Yale University Press, 2010.

Mercer, Joyce Ann, and Bonnie J. Miller-McLemore, eds. *Conundrums in Practical Theology*. Leiden: Brill, 2016.

Webber, Robert, ed. *Listening to the Beliefs of Emerging Churches*. Grand Rapids: Zondervan, 2007.

Christian Religious Education and Teaching

Astley, Jeff, Leslie J. Francis, and Colin Crowder, eds. *Theological Perspectives on Christian Education: A Reader on Theology and Christian Education.* Grand Rapids: Eerdmans, 1996.

Bass, Dorothy C., and Craig Dykstra. *For Life Abundant: Practical Theology, Theological Education, and Christian Ministry.* Grand Rapids: Eerdmans, 2008.

Fernandez, Eleazar S., ed. *Teaching for a Culturally Diverse and Racially Just World.* Eugene, OR: Cascade, 2014.

Groome, Thomas H. *Will There Be Faith? A New Vision for Educating and Growing Disciples.* New York: Harper One, 2011.

Harris, Maria, and Gabriel Moran. *Reshaping Religious Education: Conversations on Contemporary Practice.* Louisville: Westminster John Knox, 2003.

Moore, Mary Elizabeth Mullino. *Teaching from the Heart: Theology and Educational Method.* Minneapolis: Fortress, 1998.

Parrett, Gary A., S, Steve Kang, and J. I. Packer, *Teaching the Faith, Forming the Faithful: A Biblical Vision for Education in the Church.* Downers Grove, IL: IVP, 2009.

Pazmiño, Robert W. *God as Teacher: Theological Basics in Christian Education.* Grand Rapids: Baker, 1994.

Westerhoff, John. *Spiritual Life: Foundation for Preaching and Teaching.* Louisville: Westminster John Knox Press, 1994.

Media and the Arts

Bauer, Michael. *Arts Ministry: Nurturing the Creative Life of God's People.* Grand Rapids: Eerdmans, 2013.

Bausch, Michael G. *Silver Screen, Sacred Story: Using Multimedia in Worship.* Bethesda, MD: Alban Institute, 2002.

Craft, Jennifer Allen. *Placemaking and the Arts.* Downers Grove, IL: IVP, 2018.

DeBoer, Lisa J. *Visual Arts in the Worshiping Church.* Grand Rapids: Eerdmans, 2016.

Dyer, John. *People of the Screen: How Evangelicals Created the Digital Bible and How It Shapes Their Reading of Scripture.* New York: Oxford University Press, 2023.

Hess, Mary E. *Engaging Technology in Theological Education.* New York: Rowman & Littlefield, 2005.

Price, David H. *In the Beginning Was the Image: Art and the Reformation Bible.* Oxford: Oxford University Press, 2021.

Shaw, Susan M. *Storytelling in Religious Education*. Birmingham, AL: Religious Education Press, 1999.

Stories and Rituals

Ammerman, Nancy Tatom. *Sacred Stories, Spiritual Tribes: Finding Religion in Everyday Life*. Oxford: Oxford University Press, 2014.

Bausch, William J. *Storytelling: Imagination and Faith*. Mystic, CT: Twenty-Third, 1984.

Bell, Catherine, ed. *Teaching Ritual*. Oxford: Oxford University Press, 2007.

Murphy, Debra Dean. *Teaching That Transforms: Worship as the Heart of Christian Education*. Grand Rapids: Brazos, 2004.

The Contemporary Church

Hill, Graham. *Global Church*. Downers Grove, IL: IVP Academic, 2016.

Rogers, Andrew P. *Congregational Hermeneutics: How Do We Read?* Burlington, VT: Ashgate, 2015.

Romero, Robert Chao. *Brown Church: Five Centuries of Latina/o Social Justice, Theology, and Identity*. Downers Grove, IL: IVP, 2020.

Sargeant, Wendi. *Christian Education and the Emerging Church*. Eugene, OR: Pickwick, 2015.

Wimberly, Anne. *Soul Stories: African American Christian Education*. Nashville: Abingdon, 1994.

Prophetic Christian Formation

Brueggemann, Walter. *The Practice of Prophetic Imagination: Preaching an Emancipating Word*. Minneapolis: Fortress, 2012.

Freire, Paolo. *Pedagogy of the Oppressed*. New York: Seabury, 1973.

Mongoven, Anne Marie. *The Prophetic Spirit of Catechesis: How We Share the Fire in Our Hearts*. Mahwah, NJ: Paulist Press, 2000.

Recinos, Harold J. *Good News from the Barrio: Prophetic Witness for the Church*. Louisville: Westminster John Knox, 2006.

Sanborn, Hugh, ed. *The Prophetic Call: Celebrating Community, Earth, Justice, and Peace*. St. Louis: Chalice, 2004.

Theobaris, Liz. *Always with Us? What Jesus Really Said about the Poor*. Grand Rapids: Eerdmans, 2017.

One God Too Many

As the leader of his community of refugees, Yohanan son of Kareah had faced tough decisions before. Before fleeing from Judah to Egypt, he had courted Jeremiah, though others had accused the prophet of being a Babylonian collaborator, only to have his overture blow up in his face. As he often reminded himself and anyone else who would listen, against great odds and the opposition of pro-Babylonians like Baruch son of Neriah and Jeremiah himself, he had led the stragglers, including the reluctant prophet, across the rugged northern Sinai to a strange land, settling in the eastern Nile delta in Tahpanhes, the capital of northern Egypt.

It had been a long, sleepless night. After yesterday's assembly of the people, he now faced the toughest decision of his career. As leader of the Judahites living in Egypt, he must decide whether his people, especially the women, would continue to offer incense to the Queen of Heaven, who they believed had protected their travels, their husbands and children, and the nation as a whole. To allow them to continue, however, meant that Yohanan must ignore the oracle of a prophet who had always been right before and who was the ultimate survivor of political disaster.

Jeremiah has demanded that the community stop worshiping the Queen of Heaven altogether in order to avoid Yahweh's continued wrath. On the other hand, in the assembly, both the women whom Jeremiah had attacked for burning incense to the Queen of Heaven and their indignant husbands refused to listen to the prophet, for various reasons that Yohanan could not dismiss out of hand if he wished to continue to

---

A prior version of this case appeared in Mark W. Hamilton, "One God Too Many: Jeremiah and the Worship of the Queen of Heaven (Jeremiah 44)," *Journal for Case Teaching* 14 (2004): 11–21.

lead his community. Nor could he disregard those who still supported Jeremiah, those always quoting the book of the law King Josiah had found in the Temple, those always chattering about our history of sin, punishment, repentance, and salvation.

I should have left Jeremiah back home, he mumbled, to no one in particular. I dragged him here because a man like that who always gets out of scrapes has to have divine protection of some kind. But now he claims to have a revelation from Yahweh condemning us for what we've always done. If Yahweh really is the only God, why didn't our ancestors say so? Why do we sing the psalm, "Before the gods I sing your praise" or call Yahweh "God of gods"? (Ps. 138:1; 136:2). Why do we speak of Yahweh and his Asherah?[1] How can I tell my mother that her mother and her mother were idolaters, that our greatest rulers were no different than these damn Egyptians and their loud-mouthed pharaohs?[2] How can I disrupt the lives of my people in this strange land more than they've already experienced?

In a few hours, when the assembly met again, he would have to answer these questions, for himself and others. Whatever he decided would have profound implications for his community, his status as leader, and the life of his family.

Stepping Backward

The Babylonian sack of Jerusalem[3] led to a refugee crisis in the region as many were deported to slave markets in Syria and Mesopotamia, others fled to the Transjordan (to Ammon or Moab) or to Egypt, and still others attempted to reestablish life in the homeland. The Babylonians had appointed as governor the nobleman Gedaliah son of Ahiqam son of Shaphan, leader of a family long supportive of Jeremiah and even earlier of the reforms of Josiah. Gedaliah's reign was short-lived, however, for in the turmoil of the postwar world, he had

1. See the inscriptions from Kuntillet Ajrud and Khirbet el-Qom; and the discussion in Ziony Zevit, *The Religions of Ancient Israel: A Synthesis of Parallactic Approaches* (London: Continuum, 2001), 350–438.

2. See the pun on Pharaoh Hophra's name in Jer 46:17. The Hebrew *he'ebir* ("he missed") apparently puns on Hophra's Egyptian name *w'ḥ-ib-r'* (possibly pronounced *Wa-ib-re*). His name also appears in a more normal Hebraized form in 44:30.

3. In the summer of 586 BCE.

been assassinated by renegades playing on anti-Babylonian senti-
ment. In such times of hardship and political uncertainty, responsible,
resourceful leaders like Yohanan must act in unprecedented ways.[4]
He had moved his people.

Streams of refugees headed to Egypt, carrying what they could,
defying the proverbial admonition, "you shall not go that way again"
(Deut 17:16) to escape the storm troopers from the north. Egypt had
welcomed them, and in Egypt they would stay. Some sailed down the
Nile all the way to Yeb (or Elephantine) on the Egyptian border at the
First Cataract, where they joined other western Semites to build a new
life as soldiers and traders. With them went Yahweh and his consorts,
Anathbethel and Eshembethel.[5]

Along the way, some foreigners had also come to the worship of
Yahweh, finding in him aid and comfort. Yohanan remembered his
encounter with the Rashites, whose ancestors had been deported by the
Assyrians from the Far East to Bethel in the land of Israel. Their psalm
stuck in his head: "Mar is our God; Horus-Yaho our bull is with us.
May the lord of Bethel answer us tomorrow!"[6] Quite a little jingle, that
one! At the time he had thought, Yahweh, our God, has acted among
foreigners, who recognized that he was another representation of their
ancestral deity Mar. How wonderful to know that we all worship the
same God, though in many forms.

But Yohahan hardly has time for theological speculations now. There
are houses to build, latrines to dig, food to grow. His people need the
protection of any deity they can get, and they need to build a new life
for themselves. Hasn't even Jeremiah himself written the deportees to
Babylon instructing them to settle down in their new land (Jer 29:4–23)?
But how far can we go and still hold onto our identity, Yohanan wondered? We've always worshipped the Queen of Heaven, in spite of what
Jeremiah and his colleagues say about our past.

4. On the aftermath of the siege, see 2 Kgs 25:22–26. On the Shaphan family, see
2 Kgs 22; Jer 26, 36, and 39; but see the discussion in *HALOT*, 1633–34.

5. See Cowley 22 = C 3.15:126–28 in Bezalel Porten and Ada Yardeni, *Textbook of
Aramaic Documents from Ancient Egypt*, vol. 3: *Literature, Accounts, Lists* (Winona Lake:
Eisenbrauns, 1993).

6. Papyrus Amherst 63, col. 11. See the translation of Richard Steiner in *COS* 1:309–27.

In his darker moments, Yohanan wondered what it meant to be Yahweh's people when the deity himself has cast us off. What did it mean to sing Yahweh's songs in a strange land?

Seeking Consensus

Perhaps the best solution is to strive for continuity, to find the right precedents. But what were they? Ignoring long-standing practices of pious people in the interest of an unproven theory of Yahweh's nature surely is a bad idea for people already traumatized by exile. Yohanan remembered what people used to call Jeremiah, "Magor Misaviv, Terror all around" (Jer 20:10). What a bitter man, always condemning us for our sins, constantly predicting we'd fall. No wonder they say Nebuchadnezzar made sure no one killed him after the holy city fell; siding with the winner always pays! Still, he was right about the incompetence of our politicians; in fact, he's always been right about everything, the lucky son of a . . .

Before he could finish his thought, Yohanan's wife Mibtahiah entered the room.

He remembered the time years before when his father had announced that he was to marry her. Yohanan had been glad: she was a charming girl, fourteen and quite beautiful with her long neck and slightly round belly like a heap of golden wheat. And she was sensible, the sort of woman who "extended her arms to the poor and clothed her family in scarlet" (Prov 31:20–21). There was no scarlet here in Egypt, and she was thinner and grayer now, but still the old beauty remained.

"What are we to do, dear?" she began hesitantly.

Mibtahiah knew that though Yohanan could be decisive when necessary, his was a hard decision. Yesterday's assembly of the people had been painful. Jeremiah is obviously a great man, but his views seem implausible to Mibtahiah, who had prayed fervently to the Queen of Heaven during all four of her pregnancies, just as her mother had before her. And she had four beautiful children as tokens of the goddess's blessing.

"As I see it," she continued in a near whisper, "Jeremiah has gone too far. He says that Yahweh destroyed Jerusalem because our ancestors worshipped the Queen of Heaven and other gods. Even our greatest kings irritated God by doing that. Which kings he didn't say—David,

Solomon, Hezekiah? I don't know how he can say that. And you saw how he tried to blame us women for all this: 'Why are you doing a great evil against yourself?' (Jer 44:7) indeed!"

Yohanan slowly lifted his head from his hands.

"You know how prophets are. They always overstate things to make a point. Jeremiah loves these savage speeches of his. But still, he has a point, right? We *are* here in the very place Moses took our ancestors from; it's as if our entire history has been reversed, but with no Passover this time. Jerusalem is a wasteland. King Zedekiah, the poor old fool, is dead; his sons are dead. Surely this didn't happen without Yahweh's permission! And it happened just like Jeremiah predicted years and years before. You have to give him that. He stood up to kings all those years predicting this mess. He did tell us to worship Yahweh alone and stop trusting in the temple as if it were a talisman. I can't just ignore him now. But I also can't ignore everything we've done and believed all these years. I really don't know what to say today."

Then, almost as an afterthought, he turned to her and became the uncertain young man she had married: "What do you think I should do?"

Mibtahiah pulled away, though not too far away.

"True enough, Yohanan. But Jeremiah's timing is off, isn't it? I liked what somebody said yesterday: 'When we offered drink offerings to the Queen of Heaven, blessed be she, we ate enough bread, and we were well off, and evil we did not see.' Isn't that a nice touch: 'evil we did not see'? Very poetic I think. 'But since we stopped offering sacrifices to the Queen of Heaven, we have lacked everything, and by sword and famine have we been consumed.' How can you argue with that? If Yahweh really wanted us to stop worshipping his wife, and I don't see for one moment why he would want that, wouldn't he have let us know that earlier? I think Jeremiah's mind was made up in advance. He thinks only the people who went to Babylon will be the remnant of Israel."

"Oh, Mibtahiah. Who knows what Yahweh wants and why? Maybe Jeremiah's timing is off. Maybe ours is. The gods can do anything they want, and we can misunderstand them whichever way we go. If Yahweh is the only God, and I worship the Queen of Heaven, then I'm a fool and an idolater. An insolent man, they'll call me, for certain. And if she is our goddess, and Jeremiah is wrong or lying or just trying to kill us off so someone else will be the remnant of Israel, and I listen to him, then I'm also a fool because she won't protect us in this strange land! Maybe this is just some marital discord up in Heaven, and I'm caught in the middle. But I have to make a decision, don't I? The people have always looked to me for guidance. I'm their leader. With Yahweh's help—and as you always remind me, with Astarte's help—I brought them here. Without me, they'll lose our traditions for certain. Already they're marrying Egyptians. Did you see your sister's grandson Ptah-ezri the other day? What would your grandmother say about a kid named for an Egyptian god?"

Mibtahiah brushed Yohanan's cheek with her hand in that tender way of hers.

"You'll make the right call. You always do. I will pray to the Queen for you. She will talk to her husband Yahweh about this. It will be all right. You'll see."

Yohanan left to meet the elders, still not sure what he would do. Today might make the difference in the history of his community, and the weight of the decision weighed heavily on his shoulders. Who truly is God? Who are we?

For Further Reading

Carroll, Robert. *Jeremiah*. Old Testament Library. Louisville: Westminster John Knox, 1986.

Holladay, William. *Jeremiah*. 2 vols. Hermeneia; Minneapolis: Fortress, 1989.

Keel, Othmar, and Christoph Uehlinger. *Gods, Goddesses, and Images of God*. Minneapolis: Fortress, 1998.

Lundbom, Jack. *Jeremiah*. 3 vols. to date, through chap. 36. Anchor Bible 21A–C. New York: Doubleday, 1998–2004.

Sharp, Carolyn. *Prophecy and Ideology in Jeremiah: Struggles for Authority in the Deutero-Jeremianic Prose*. London: Continuum, 2003.

Smith, Mark S. *The Early History of God: Yahweh and the Other Deities in Ancient Israel*. 2nd ed. Grand Rapids: Eerdmans, 2002.

Stulman, Louis. *Order amid Chaos: Jeremiah as Symbolic Tapestry*. Sheffield: Sheffield Academic Press, 1998.

Zevit, Ziony. *The Religions of Ancient Israel: A Synthesis of Parallactic Approaches*. London: Continuum, 2001.

Teaching Notes

Goals

1. To challenge students' views of polytheists as unthinking or wicked persons, or, conversely, simplistic rejections of the biblical tradition as irremediably patriarchal.
2. To highlight the fact that the move to monotheism in ancient Israel was the result of careful theological reflection over time and that the move was neither inevitable nor necessarily more "rational" than alternatives.
3. To underscore the interrelationships among theological, economic, political, and other social forces in the decision-making of individuals in antiquity.
4. To help students understand the rhetorically loaded language of the prophetic books and thus to recognize that this rhetoric seeks to foreclose alternative understandings of the historical events it records (while at the same time making room for a reconstruction of just those alternatives).
5. To invite students to enter the ongoing Christian attempts to formulate appropriate theological language for referring to God.

Settings

This case could be used in a college or seminary classroom, particularly in an introductory course in Hebrew Bible/Old Testament, or one on the prophets, or perhaps one in comparative religion. Optimally, the case will take place in the context of a larger discussion (with lectures and readings) of Israel's ongoing discussion of the nature of Yahweh's relationship with them.

Issues

1. The nature of theological reflection, particularly in light of historical circumstances.
2. Appropriate/befitting conceptions of deity (*theoprepes*).
3. The genderedness of religious practice and religious change.
4. The development and preservation of tradition, especially in the face of massive social disruption.

5. Leadership in religious communities, especially problems arising from conflict among leaders.
6. The valorization of collective memory of past practices and personages.
7. Family relations across generations and gendered behaviors.
8. The validation/invalidation of alleged divine speech.

Design

1. Begin by asking the group to identify times when their communities have wrestled with the problem of finding appropriate language to describe God's work among them. What were the issues? How did the discussions play out? (7 minutes)
2. Have the group identify the theological issues of the case. (10 minutes)
3. Ask the group to focus on Yohanan. What other factors must he consider in decision-making for this community? (10 minutes)
4. Divide into three groups. Each group must plot a strategy for solving this problem. One group will argue the position of the Queen of Heaven people. Another will argue Jeremiah's Yahweh-alone position. The third group will seek some sort of viable compromise. (15 minutes)
5. Bring groups together (fish bowl) to discuss the issues in the case. (15 minutes)
6. Force the group to vote on which position they believe to have been best argued. (3 minutes)
7. Discuss the process of theological reflection. What made the issues so difficult? What values in our own minds made the case difficult? (15 minutes)

Index of Subjects

ethical reflection, 6, 33, 47, 119, 122, 128, 142, 152
Eucharist, 21, 24, 59, 61, 64–69, 73, 80–82, 152, 154, 157

fasting, 140
filtering, 38–41
Freire, Paolo, 146
fundamentalism, 9, 13, 16, 70, 143, 148

Gilgamesh, 29
Global North, 3, 8, 138, 140, 154
global pandemic. *See* COVID-19
Global South, 3, 138
God: attributes of, 43–45, 49, 86–87; as benefactor, 1, 4, 8–9, 13, 16, 35, 38, 42, 44–45, 62, 65, 68, 77, 88, 109, 116, 130, 137, 139, 145; and the Bible, 9, 12, 13, 15–16, 54–55; and the church, 111; as creator, 9, 110, 127, 147; faith in, 2; and the gods, 165–70; and humanity, 6, 11, 13, 22, 28, 103, 108, 121, 154; and Israel, 12, 31, 34–36, 38, 41, 46–47, 60, 62, 68, 104, 151, 153, 157; and Jesus Christ, 9, 15, 25, 42, 67, 82, 157; as literary character, 105, 125–28; love for, 19, 86; and morality, 45, 63, 119; and prayer, 1, 41, 68, 74–77, 132; promises of, 12; and punishment, 106–8; and revelation, 110; and sin, 39n11, 130; speech about, 46, 52–54, 150–51; as teacher, 66; transcendent, 15; and transformation, 149; ways of, 89–103; and wisdom, 119–20, 125, 133,

135, 142, 144; worship of, 63–65, 68, 73, 77–78, 82, 110, 134, 141, 157
Groome, Thomas, 22, 147n8, 150

Hall, Douglas John, 143
Hanukkah, 61
heritage, ix, 7, 97
hermeneutics of suspicion, 4
Holocaust, 1–2
Holy Spirit, 12, 81
honesty, 10, 23, 32, 108, 128, 141, 151–52

identity, 7, 34–35, 72, 142, 167
Iliad, 29
imagination, 3, 34, 47, 53, 75, 94, 103–4, 146, 158, 159; of God, 13; of prophets, 16; and tradition, 85–89
inspiration, 13–16
Islam, 14–15, 75n14

Jennings, Willie James, 98
Jerusalem, 38, 64, 74, 91, 166, 168–69
Jesus: and apostles, 3, 31, 41; authority of, 16; and the church, 7, 17, 42, 44–45, 77, 129, 131–32, 142; as cosmic Christ, 41; death of, 48, 65–66, 68–69, 78; enthroned, 42; faith in, 13–15; as interpreter of Scripture, 38, 123; and Israel, 42, 44, 49, 60, 75–76, 87, 153, 157; as messiah, 104; and prayer, 75–76, 81–82, 132, 154; preaching about, 40–41, 51; as revelation, 14; as the Word, 16, 25; work of, 9, 14,

Index of Scripture